Max, V and Me

The Early Years

Book 1

Chapters 1 to 21

Max, V and Me

The Early Years

BASED ON TRUE EVENTS.

*My Tormented Life's Spiritual,
Paranormal and Supernatural Journey,
Seeking Healing, Acceptance, and Peace*

Charm Heart

Library of Congress Control Number: 2023907406
ISBN: Hardcover   979-8-3694-9112-6
                 Softcover   979-8-3694-9111-9
                 eBook   979-8-3694-9110-2

Visit - Charm Heart: https://httpswwwmaxvandme.com/.
Correspondence - Charm Heart: maxvandme@hotmail.com

Print information available on the last page.

Rev. date: 07/13/2023

To order additional copies of this book, contact:
Xlibris
AU TFN: 1 800 844 927 (Toll Free inside Australia)
AU Local: (02) 8310 8187 (+61 2 8310 8187 from outside Australia)
www.Xlibris.com.au
Orders@Xlibris.com.au
850558

Table Of Content

In loving memory of my Dad.

Acknowledgements

A huge THANK YOU to
my guide, Max & my guardian, V.
You are both forever in my thoughts and prayers.

A special THANK YOU to everyone who has
supported me throughout my life.

My husband Leslie, children & grandchildren.
My parents, sister & brother.
My closest family members & cousins.
My best friend's forever; Neena, Marisha & Antoinette.

Especially to . . . Mom and Antoinette, as they have
spent years assisting me, by reading, scrutinising
& editing the series of Max, V and Me books.

Introduction

*T*his book is based on true events that have occurred in my life. It is about my gifts and the paranormal encounters I had experienced. There were incidents which occurred that I have come to know about that involved me. I started drafting this book when I was in my early teens. I am now in my mid-fifties. It's been a long tiresome journey. I've stopped and started writing multiple times throughout my life, adding more memories as time elapsed.

At first, I wrote with the intention of publishing a handful of copies only for my children and grandchildren, which they could give to future generations in our family to read. This book will hopefully enable them to understand their gifts and what they can do to help them cope. I do this by explaining what has happened to me and what I chose to do with my gifts to find peace.

These supernatural gifts have been passed down from my ancestors onto some family members through birth. I have the gift but not everyone has it. All three of my biological children do, to some extent. I am absolutely sure it's been given to at least one of my grandchildren.

I realised, while writing this book this time around, I can help others in this world who are struggling to cope with their special gifts. This book explains my early life and what I can do, which is photograph soul orbs. I see, hear and can talk to spirits. I sometimes dream of my past lives and on occasions, future events.

My guide, Max and my guardian, V, accompany me through my life and are with me every step of the way. I hope telling the world is not my downfall. That it does not have negative repercussions on my family and friends.

Please be kind and understanding readers. That is why I have changed our names, in the hope of protecting the ones I love. I have kept most of the locations true. I have not written this book to offend anyone. Sincere apologies beforehand if it does.

At this time, I would like to take this opportunity to express my thoughts on plagiarism. Multiple people who authored a book like this one, have been accused of plagiarism. Please understand that Max, V and I do not in any way want anyone to think we have copied them. If what I have written in this book is similar to what someone else has written or said, we apologise relentlessly. We do not want to step on anyone's toes. Please understand there is only so many ways to explain a common occurrence or an experience. It's the same supernatural or paranormal subjects that a substantial number of authors are writing about.

Max's, V's and my opinions are our own. We do not want to put anyone down. We are just trying to get these incidents we have experienced out into the world. Therefore, my friends, please take these written words as an acknowledgement of what you have said, things either Max, V or I believe to be true, as well as you do. These things, we have lived through together and also want to record it in our own perspectives.

Remember, other people may not have the same perspectives as my own. These are some of the spirit people's, Max's, V's or my feelings. We are reminiscing and I am recording our conversations and memories. I do not agree with everything that Max, V or what dead people have told me and about which I have written. Usually having to experience things first before I am a believer. However, I enjoy the debates and the stories told and I am curious on the validation points made. That is the reason it is in this book.

Disclaimer: Even though each story is based on true events and real people, in some incidents; I may have cut the scenes a lot shorter, changed the person's identity, character and place, as to not offend or to hurt anyone, and to avoid getting sued *(due to past threats made)*. I am still telling the truth but in a round-about way or have given a much sutler account, to protect myself.

Our books and videos should not be construed as professional advice, they are merely a presentation of facts as we understand them. We are not professionals, and you should seek the services of a professional if you believe that you are a victim of supernatural behaviours and, or spiritual behaviours and, or abuse of any kind and, or experience circumstances, such as those written or portrayed by us, Max, V or me (Charm). The facts presented in the Max, V and Me books and videos are not indicative of my (Charm's) personal opinion, and I do not always agree with the outcome, people, or stories or judgements of any interaction Laws, case law, ordinances, policies, legal doctrine, and all other jurisprudence is subject to the interpretation of the court. Any legal topics covered in the Max, V and Me books and videos, including podcasts and any other recordings, are designed to be educational and informative, and should not serve as professional or legal advice under any circumstances. The contents of this book and all recordings is in no way intended to provoke, incite, or shock the reader or viewer. This book and all recordings, be it written, visual and, or in audio format, was created to bring awareness and to educate citizens about occurrences that had happened in Max, V and Charm Heart's lifetimes or about occurrences that had happened around Charm Heart's family, friends or acquaintances that involve her in some way.

Come back with me on my early life's journey. I invite you to follow along with the songs, free (in 2023) on YouTube. I have selected most in lyrics form; they are music videos. The music expresses my inner feelings and emotions, much more than I ever could describe in this book. It is selected from my lifetime's favorite songs list. It may not be from the same period that I am writing about, that occurred in my life.

The best place to start is in the beginning.

My Baby Photo

Chapter 1

Gift

*F*or as long as I can remember, I've heard V's and Max's voices in my head. I think they've always been there. I was told, when I was a baby, I was always alert, responsive and hardly ever cried. My Aunt, Helen Chance, was extremely attached to me; she would come over all the time and look after me. It was because she could hear the voices that spoke to me.

When she carried or touched me, I could hear the voices in her head, whispering to her and she'd respond immediately. The voices were noticed only by us; they said a lot of foul words and told Auntie Helen off all the time and would attack her, if she didn't comply with their requests.

At an exceptionally early age, Max and V told me not to tell anyone about the voices or about them.

"People wouldn't understand right now. You need to learn more to understand why you can hear us . . . but don't worry, one day people will know our names," V said.

Therefore, I kept them secret. It was okay with them for me to tell Hector, my teddy bear. I loved watching *Hector's House* on TV with my teddy. They looked so similar. I guess that's how he inherited his name. As my only friend, I treasured Hector. He had beautiful round brown plastic eyes. He was covered in soft curly light brown fur and had a black plastic nose. I used to feed him porridge and play with him constantly. He was my confidant and when not in my arms, his head would rest on my pillow until I joined him to snuggle at night.

We were living in the middle apartment of a three-story mid-terraced house on Harvest Road in Queens Park, Brent. I used to see and hear telepathically spirits in semi-transparent forms on a daily basis, see tiny balls of dancing lights, which are soul orbs and other entities by that age. The tall house was one of many, all strung together along the side of a busy road. All five of us—my parents, brother, sister and I—slept in one bedroom. Our living room was next to our bedroom. We would enter it via a narrow hallway. This hallway had steps connected to the upper and lower floors as well as every room my family used in that house. We didn't have much privacy.

Two other families shared our abode, one below and the other above us. The front door was at the bottom of a steep flight of steps. Our restroom, bathroom and kitchen, which our parents kept locked, were on the opposite side of the house to the bedroom and living room; we had to walk past the steps, through the hallway to get to them. Our dwelling areas were split in two.

Mom looked after us well. She kept all the rooms and communal hallway spotlessly clean and neat. She cooked wonderful meals and read us books, played card games and played puzzles with us. Dad, we didn't see much; he worked a night shift at *Kodak* and brought in a steady wage. Mom did her best keeping us kids quiet while he slept during the day and she didn't want to upset the neighbors, who surrounded us on all sides, with us playing and our noise. We spent a lot of time in the kitchen on the other side of the house, away from

Dad or if it were not raining, Mom would take us to Queens Park, which was just a short walk across the street.

***

I would insist on wearing my favorite white shirt, knee-length socks, purple skirt and jacket to see the balloon man who was always at the bandstand. I used to pray that I would be the one picked out of all the kids to help him make balloon hats, animals and designs. Many times, sitting on the steps watching him was a little spirit boy. He was about nine years old. Max told me his name was Timmy; he was from the light and the balloon man's son.

Max said, "Charm girl, he visits his daddy a lot because his dad misses him."

Timmy followed us home once. He knew I could see him, but he didn't say a word to me. He just smiled, looked down at his shoes and smiled again. At our front door, while Mom was fiddling in her handbag, he waved at me goodbye then turned and walked away, back across the road towards the bandstand. He disappeared when Mom opened the front door with her key. I was extremely upset that a little boy died. I was so touched that he still loved his dad so much. I could feel this boy's sadness.

I thought that I would die too. I was fearful to die. It was scary to know other souls know exactly what you did when living and worse, what you had done when you've died! I wouldn't talk to Max or V for the rest of that day. V tried to comfort me. I couldn't understand why the little boy didn't want to go to heaven. I was told I could talk to him and ask him to wait in heaven for his dad. I agreed. It so happened; I never saw this little soul again.

"Chiquitita" - Abba (Lyrics) (Tiktok Song)

Max's Orb

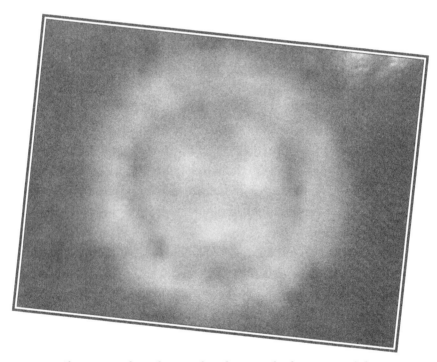

This is an enlarged copy of a photograph of Max in orb form.
Max is pleased to make your acquaintance.

Chapter 2

Max, V and Me

I was around four or five years old when I actually saw Max for the first time. As you enter our bedroom on Harvest Road, to the right was a long wall with a square window. This window was unusually situated to the left of this wall, nearest to the corner. Our bunk bed was placed against that long blank part of the wall and the ladder at the end of the bunk bed nearly touched the windowsill.

Each night Anthony, my brother, would climb the ladder and sleep on the top bunk. I slept below him. Mom and Dad's queen-sized bed was butted up seamlessly against our bunk bed. Hector, my teddy and I would sleep on the bottom bunk, nearest to the wall, next to my baby sister, Theresa. Then Mom would sleep next to her. When Dad was home on his off days from shift work, he slept on the end of the bed next to the bedroom door.

I remember lying on the bottom bunk. I was flat on my back with my hands clasped loosely together behind my head. My Mom had just bathed me, my hair smelt sweet. It felt like silk in between my fingertips. My Mom always used to brush my hair until it shined. At night, she would tuck me into bed and say prayers with me. She always used to kiss me and my teddy Hector, whose job it was to snuggle up beside me. Blankets were pulled up to the little bear's chin, my arm around him, his head and floppy ears cradled on my chest.

That particular night, I listened in the dark to V, who was, at that moment, a bodyless orb of energy. She was telling me about the dancing lights I always used to see before I went to sleep. She would describe the person talking to me, who was inside them. The stories she told me, I had heard many times before, so I knew the endings of most of them by heart. I still loved hearing them over and over. I cannot remember all the previous conversations with V. These were some of a few early memories that have stuck with me to this day. She used to tell me stories about Max's younger sister and her baby girl who was the same age as my little sister, Theresa.

This day was different. There were no stories that night. V told me I will see Max for the first time. I recall thinking he was going to come out of the wall, just like the other dancing orbs of light. A white or grey smoky figure or it would appear like faceless eyes that used to visit me a lot. I was happier when V explained to me that I would see him clearly when I close my eyes. She told me not to be afraid because he would look different.

"I won't leave you and you will still hear my voice until you feel safe," she said.

I was so excited that Max was coming to visit me. I closed my eyes, now thinking I would see a tiny little person like Tom Thumb or Thumbelina. I was instantly afraid when a man's figure appeared. He was sitting close and facing me, crossed-legged on my Mom and Dad's side of their queen-sized bed.

He was dark-skinned, in his mid-thirties. I will never forget what he said to me.

"Hello, my darling little girl. I'm Max and I come in peace. You know my voice, don't you? Jesus sent me to guide you and we are going to be best friends. I'm so happy that you can see me now, Charm. I've waited a long time for this day to come."

I clung Hector close; nervously, I asked Max, "Are you a good boy or a bad boy?"

"Cha Girl, I love Jesus, you know this, right? So that makes me a good boy. I say, *'Our Lord's Prayer.'* I know Jesus well. It's one of mine and His favorites," he said.

I could easily distinguish between Max and V's voices. Max sounded masculine. He had a Jamaican accent and was very funny. V's voice was feminine. Her accent was British. She can be quite serious at times. Max and V proceeded to recite a prayer similar to the way my Mom often said it but with a few more words added. It was the *"Our Father"* prayer.

His voice was clear. He spoke softly, then he spoke in my head telepathically, as if whispering.

"I also like the prayer you say to me, Charm, *'Angel of God, my guardian dear to whom God's love commits me here. Ever this night, be at my side, to light, to guard, to rule and guide . . . .'* I am here now, my girl. I'm here to guide you."

"What does a guide do?" I asked inquisitively.

"Girl, heaven has put me here to keep you on your life's path, to show you the way, as it is all written for me on the palms of your hands. The finer details are within your fingertips. It's like a road map for me to follow. This helps me to guide you."

He could see I looked confused, so Max continued, "No two palm prints are exactly the same and every fingerprint is different, my girl. I can read that. It's like my 'go-to book.' Everyone has a different path. It is written on palms and fingertips. Understand, Charm?"

"Um, where's my palms on my hands? What does my feet do? I have lines on them too! What's a road map and a go-to book? Max, what is your job again?" I shot questions back at him.

"Woo-wee, I see I'm going to have to take this slower, little one. I'm sorry!" Max chuckled.

From that day, Max appeared periodically every day and played games with me. As he spoke, pictures would appear in my head when

I closed my eyes. As the years went by, I saw pictures, recognisable numbers, and letters flash before my eyes. This would happen even when they were open. Max taught me what symbols and signs meant, different words such as when I saw a flower flash. It meant *I love you.*

Then I started seeing scenes similar to short movie clips or acts, to enable me to figure out secret messages Max would make up. It was a fun game and I loved it. Every night I would pray with my Mom, then when she had left the room, Max, V and I would pray to God together for protection for all my family. We would pray mainly, to praise God Himself. *(To whom at times, Max and V would refer to God as "The Source").*

I have always been able to converse with Max and V telepathically. It was not unusual for me. I thought everyone did it. I used to think everyone saw the white balls of light because everyone has a few hanging around them. I don't recall asking why I saw or heard these things; I suppose it would be like asking,

"Why do I hear birds singing?"

It's a stupid question to ask. It was a normal thing for me to hear voices and see things, so I didn't question it.

Bedtime stories were told to me nightly; they were about our past lives and important bullet points during them that had occurred. They told me stories of long ago, about when we lived on different planets. I wanted to know about heaven and how we got to earth in this lifetime. I wanted to know about my birth. I can remember V and Max floating above as they told their tales and set the scenes from before I was born and when I was too young to remember.

"When You Believe" – Whitney Huston and Mariah Carey (Lyrics)

Chapter 3

At Departure

While looking at them one at a time, I asked, "You'll have my back, right, V and Max?"

"Don't worry, Charm, we'll be waiting for you on the other side," V replied.

"We'll see you at 8:05 in the evening, girl, yes! We're keeping an eye on the countdown. Okay, we had better get ready now. We're next," Max said.

We got up and stood in front of a large circular entrance on the tall wall. It was big enough for us all to step into it side-by-side. The circle opening was sheer, shimmering and glassy, randomly moving like white silver-outlined fog, bellowing hazy clouds. No smell or sound was detected, just a tingly, static sensation came over us all as we approached. We felt as if we were slightly being drawn towards it and out of the small white room, like magnets coming together when held closely.

Our silvery-coloured clothes were shiny and loose-fitting. We all wore the same thing—floor-length lightweight, thin, and silky-to-the-touch robes, V-neck with long baggy sleeves similar to choir boys—and wore nothing else. The only difference was, as V and I had long hair, we wore our locks tied up high in a ponytail with thin silvery elasticated ribbons.

"Positions, please," echoed throughout the small room.

We stepped forward and took our positions side-by-side on luminous squares on the warm glowing floor. There was one for each of us, many squares all in a line. We chose to stand somewhere in the middle of the line, facing the now-gleaming opening. Now feeling the pulling sensation of our bodies getting stronger as we stood hand in hand and waited, I glanced at the chairs we were sitting on behind us about ten feet away. I realised two more people were occupying them. They were dressed like us and were waiting for their turn to go through the circle.

I looked at Max on my left and asked him, "How long have you been training together to accompany me, Max?"

"Fifteen, my girl."

"So, this is the 16th lifetime, seriously?"

"Yes, it's a long time coming. Let's do this, girls!" he replied energetically with a fist pump while looking at us with a beaming smile.

"We'll give it our best shot," V said.

I turned right to look at V, holding her hand tighter. She continued speaking while looking at me and smiling.

"We'll always be with you even if you don't talk to us, okay, Charm?"

"Okay. Thanks, guys. I understand," I said, squeezing their hands.

A voice echoed loudly around us, saying, "It's time. You will all be raised and will be drawn through the gate together. Prepare yourselves for 16 June 1966, 20:05 on earth. Good luck."

I clung hold of their hands as we were raised about two feet off the ground on the luminous squares.

"Sixteen will be our lucky number then," I said excitedly to them as we all looked forward at the fog.

"Sixteen, perfect. Don't worry, sweetheart, your body is strong and healthy. It's time that you got back into it. Try to remember that you must tell everyone to give them hope. Okay, let's pray!" V said excitedly.

"From a Distance" – Bette Midler (lyrics)

"Remember… today is the tomorrow you worried about yesterday."

Dale Carnegiel

Chapter 4

Birth

I immediately felt colder. I was wet and came out of my mother screaming.

"Congratulations, Mrs. Sweets! You have a beautiful baby girl," the doctor said as he cut my umbilical cord and handed me naked, slimy and bloody to the nurse.

"Welcome to the world, baby girl. I have someone here who is anxious to meet you. Meet your mummy!" the nurse said as she wrapped me comfortably in a clean soft white towel and placed me in my mother's outstretched arms.

"Oh wow! She's perfect. She has brown eyes like mine," Mom said, bringing me back in for another cuddle.

"I need to take her to clean her up for you while your doctor finishes up. Is that all right, Mrs. Sweets?"

"Thank you. Yes, alright," Mom replied.

"Please note the time and height, weight, um . . . in the correct spots on the form this time, Mavis, 7 pounds 6 ounces, at 20:05 on

16-6-66," the nurse said, sneering at her new assistant, who was fiddling through forms and cards with a pen in her mouth.

"The pink card, dear, the pink one. Pink for girls, blue for boys, please try to remember, dear," the nurse said, becoming irritated while rubbing my face with a clean white towel.

She started to wrap me up after wiping off my body, then wrapped me tighter in a thin pink blanket so I couldn't move my arms or legs, with only my face exposed.

"Now, Mrs. Sweets, do you have a name for this little bundle of joy?" the nurse asked.

"No, we haven't thought of a name for her yet," Mom replied.

"Baby Sweets, with an 's,' Mavis, please," the nurse said as she looked over her assistant's shoulder at what she was writing.

I was back in my Mom's arms; she was sitting up now and cradled me softly while putting me to her breast. I latched on immediately; it was thirsty work being born; you know!

"I see you've done this before," the doctor said while washing his hands and smiling at my Mom.

"Yes, Anthony, my son, is a year old now. Thanks, everyone. I couldn't have done this without you all," Mom replied proudly to everyone in the room, beaming with a huge grin.

"Well, my dear, you have your hands full now, two kids, under one! Now let's get someone to take you to the ward," the nurse said while quickly clearing up the soiled sheets from the bottom of the bed and replacing that area with a crisp clean white one.

"Mave, please call down to the ward and get the Sweets family settled in there now. They are ready to go," the doctor said while writing up some paperwork on his clipboard.

The nurse was busily cleaning up and arranging the room, she said hurriedly, "Mrs. Sweets, Mavis will bring you the phone to call your husband. You have at least ten days in hospital, my dear, so rest up as much as possible and don't be surprised if your little son has difficulty coming to you or forgets you. This happens to many mothers leaving their children for so long. If you have any questions or concerns, the maternity nurses on your ward will assist you. Don't be afraid to talk to them. Someone will be here to take you to the ward soon." She said, as she collected up all of the paperwork from the little white desk near the door.

She left the room with the doctor. Her assistant wheeled the phone over to Mom. We were not alone in the room for long. We were soon taken up to a bright and warm hospital ward, which had many other women and babies on beds. It was two rows of beds, twelve new Moms in the room. After giving me a sponge bath and changing me into some new clothes, Mom took me into the nursery. She left me in the care of some other nurses while she showered.

Nestled and wrapped tightly in a blanket, Mom had placed me in a small transparent plastic cot. It was there that I noticed V and Max in the form of tiny balls of lights. Their orbs floated around me; they spoke to me telepathically.

"Your mom won't be long, sweetheart," V said to me.

"She's perfect, isn't she, Venus? Look at her little button nose and chubby cheeks. Girl, I tell you, this one's going to be a looker. Why do they name her Charm though? She looks more like a Candy to me, Candy Sweets. What do you think? Aww, girl, she's a cute one. Am I right or am I right?" Max chuckled.

"Max, we have our work cut out for us. She's gorgeous, yes, but this little one's life plan is complicated. We have to keep on our toes cos they will try to stop her any chance they get. It's up to us, Max. We must keep her on her path. She will fight us every step of the way. Look, her mother is coming back."

"Girl, it will be okay. We're both more than ready. Charm will bring hope to thousands. We'll all complete our missions in her lifetime. Life would be boring for souls like us if it were easy. So, let's face those challenges head on. We'll do it together, one at a time."

"Together, Max," V replied proudly.

Mom returned refreshed. Her brown hair styled in a long, neat bun at the back of her head. You can see the clips in a line on the bun holding it skillfully in place. She had pinkish lipstick on and wore large pink round-framed glasses, which matched her mid-thigh pink and white floral sleeveless dress. She didn't look like she had just given birth to me at all. Her figure snapped back right away to a pretty, five feet four inches, slender, 22-year-old woman.

Mom's nature was gentle, kind and affectionate. She was an organised, immaculate, clean and tidy person. Empowered with motherhood, her protective instincts were heightened, watching my every movement and scrutinised anyone who picked me up. She was vigilant and swift to respond to my every need. Mom liked to cook. She taught herself how to crochet and knit and had made me many different styles of baby layette outfits from various patterns to dress me up in prior to my birth: matinee jackets, booties, mittens and hats for me, which were either lemon, light green or snowy white in colour, as she had no clue then of my gender.

Looking up at her while she breastfed me, her brown eyes looked lovingly into mine. She had a flawless complexion. Her dimple sank deeply in on her right cheek while showing perfectly aligned pearly whites. She smiled gleefully at me. Normally, she spoke with a pleasant soft voice to everyone, but when up close and holding me, she would whisper in comforting tones.

"My darling, your Daddy will be coming to see you tomorrow and I can't wait for you to meet your big brother. His name is Anthony, um, Tony. Sorry that your Daddy wasn't waiting to see you today, honey. He stayed as long as he could. Visiting hours here are short. You were born just as he got home. He got there by bus," Mom said.

I met my Dad the next day at 6:00 p.m. He was waiting to see Mom and me. He arrived early as usual, the first person to be lined up, with a few other men outside the maternity ward's doors, waiting impatiently for 6:00. as visiting time was strictly between 6:00 p.m. and 8:00 p.m. only every day. He was all smiles when he saw me and wanted to hold me straight away but had to wait a while until Mom had finished burping me. As Mom thumped me on my back, I heard V say softly in my head, speaking to Max,

"Her mother is radiant, she's over the moon and her dad looks so proud because he has a daughter! Look, Max, Charm's lips have changed colour. It's the same dark colour as her dad's now. She's got her mom's-coloured eyes though."

"Little one, you chose good parents. Woo-wee, my girl, yes, you sure did. Just look at him, V, you cannot wipe that smile off his face even if you tried. A real good man her dad is. They will help keep her on her path," Max added ecstatically.

Dad was 35 years old when I was born; five feet seven inches tall. He had a little bulge for a belly but otherwise quite solid and muscular. His face was a darker shade of brown than Mom's. He was handsome with light hazel eyes and really dark brown-coloured lips. His cheeks were pot-marked, little craters, like they were peppered, which made him look stern. This suited his nature as he was quiet but he was a tough man and quick to anger.

He looked good with his *Teddy Boy* hairstyle with tons of *Brylcreem*. Clean-shaven with *Old Spice* aftershave, he was always groomed well. He wore blue jeans with a loose collared white tucked-in shirt and shiny black shoes. Dad completed his style with an *Old Holborn* self-rolled cigarette, which he placed prominently balanced behind his right ear.

He was a loyal, strict and honest man. As his voice was loud, booming and intimidating, he spoke only if he had to. He always spoke his mind, bluntly and directly, sometimes swearing like a trooper if he was pissed off. Dad was a *Merchant Seaman* for years, tattoos and all. This was before he had met Mom, and I guess he never broke that way of speaking to people, which was normal to him. An obsessive TV buff, he loved his curries, sports and movies tremendously but most of all, he loved his family. We came first.

As Dad kissed me on the forehead and handed me back to Mom, he said as quietly as he could, "See you both the same time tomorrow. I'll bring Tony and your parents too. He's fine, so don't worry about him. Marge, have you got any ideas of a name for her? I was thinking about it again last night. I can't think of a really nice one for our daughter?"

"Not yet. I want her to be named after someone in our family. Definitely not Marge! Please, darling, take care of our son. Give him a huge kiss from me."

The next day Dad brought my brother, Nana and Grandpa. Tony clung hold of Dad and didn't want to go to Mom at first, which made her very unhappy, especially because it was his first birthday and she was in hospital with me.

"Name her, Charm, after your grandmother. They look so similar, the curly mop of black hair, brown eyes button nose, and those cute little cheeks," Grandpa suggested.

"I love it. What do you think, darling?" Mom asked Dad.

"I'm Alive" – Celine Dion (Lyrics)

Meet my Childhood Pets
and here are some of my
Artwork at 13 years old

Trixie my Dog

Chippy and Churpy my Budgies

Fluffy my Cat

My Four Terrapin Turtles

*"It is better to be hated for what you are,
than to be loved for what you are not."*

Andre Gide

Chapter 5

Early Family

M om and Dad migrated to England individually from India. They first met up in London, had a short engagement, got married and started a family almost immediately. My brother, Anthony (Tony), was born first, then I came along a year later, in 1966. They lovingly welcomed me into a stable working-class family. My parents, Marjorie and Ignatius Sweets, named me Charm Sweets. Dad and my grandmother looked after Anthony until Mom was discharged by the hospital and went home with me.

Four years later, Mom fell pregnant again and I soon had a baby sister named Theresa. We nicknamed her Terry. Our family was a very humble one, beatings and abuse were unheard of in our household. Only love and patience existed, with a lot of *'F and S words'* thrown in daily by Dad, which then surrounded us all.

***

Our parents only took us to the Roman Catholic churches religiously every Sunday. Dad tried his best not to curse on that day. We received all the sacraments as we took them at the appropriate ages. Dad and Mom would look beamingly and proudly at us. They would invite all the Aunties, Uncles and other family members and friends to attend the happy occasions. The pews were filled with my family members.

***

Monthly parties were the norm then. My grandparents names were Rosemary and Stephen Copper, us kids lovingly called them Nana and Grandpa. Most of the celebrations were held at their house, in West Harrow, Middlesex. Nana and Grandpa had six children, including my Mom. My Dad had a huge family in India too but at this time, we typically spent time together with my Mom's side of the family. We would have huge parties; the entire family would attend, bringing with them dishes of food for us all to share at our regular soirees. If not in West Harrow, then parties would be held at our house or at one of my other relatives.

The adults would make any excuse to have a knees-up, and we'd all have fun. Nana and Grandpa's first six-born grandchildren, Gaz, Si, Lea, Jen, my brother Tony and I, were inseparable. Many grandkids (my cousins) were born after us six. We were a solid team and played well together. I was remarkably close to Lea and Jen, Jen mostly, though, as we were the same age and would sleep over at each other's houses often.

***

One year we attended a street party together and everyone planned to come to our house. This street party was before Queen Elizabeth's Silver Jubilee. For entertainment, this party included a children's fancy-dress competition that the adults entered us kids into. My cousins, brother and I were dressed up into homemade costumes my Aunts Edna, Jane, Jess and Rose prearranged with my

Mom. Knowing this was a fancy-dress party, they organised some pretty funny get-ups for us kids to wear. I only recall a few of them.

Si was dressed in a football player costume—long socks, football boots—and he carried a football. Gaz was the sleeping man. With untidy hair, dressed in his pajamas, holding a pillow to the side of his ear. A blanket and an alarm clock was held in his other hand. It looked like he was sleeping in an upright position. Tony was dressed as the character *'Benny Hill'* on TV, usually performed, in uniform with a flat top hat and round glasses. Tony didn't like what he was wearing. After a while, Mom changed him into a football player like Si. To me, the boys' costumes were all right but not spectacular.

Jen's character, however, was 'The Lady.' She wore a pretty floppy hat, a beautiful, flowered dress and platform shoes. Makeup was applied perfectly by my Aunts. She was adorned with some gorgeous pieces of jewelry. She looked amazing. My favorite character was Lea's.

My eldest female cousin was dressed as a scruffy cleaning woman named 'Mrs. Mop.' A shabby dress and apron were put on her body. She had a dirty-looking stained scarf tied over her head, covering most of her messy hair. My Aunts made holes in Lea's wrinkled saggy stockings and put clubby-looking shoes on her, which were two sizes too big. She shuffled through the streets when she walked. It was hilarious to watch her! A fag hung loosely in her mouth, lipstick was applied without care, her face had dirty smudges and she held a mop with a stringed head and a dirty bucket. She really looked the part, brilliant!

My Mom and Aunts spent ages applying makeup to my face, styling my hair really beautifully, then dressed me in one of my long party dresses. I was incredibly pleased until they pinned page 3 of *The Sun* newspaper all over me, from my neck down to my toes. I walked around that day with photos of topless women covering my body. Boobs, boobs and more boobs, layers of paper with top models exposing their breasts covered my dress completely. I was a page 3 girl. Wow! Thanks. I won! I can't remember what my prize was, though. I guess it wasn't worth all the gawks by the men and gasps from the women in our community. My entire family did have tons of fun that day.

***

My Grandpa Stephen had a lovely singing voice and was very musical. He was extraordinarily talented and could play many musical instruments: piano, mouth organ, stringed instruments. Nana and Grandpa's house was clean, tidy, cozy and inviting. It was a normal-sized British home, with three bedrooms and a bathroom upstairs. Downstairs, though, in the living room, was my favorite place to be, as they had a black piano that stood gracefully along a wall in there. It was a prominent furniture piece I loved.

Nana was a wonderful, very pretty, intelligent, motherly, and caring woman, around five feet tall. She was of normal build with short straight salt-and-pepper side-parted hair, with always a couple of bobby pins slipped in to assist her locks from sliding onto her face. Nana loved collecting British royal memorabilia; she was very patriotic.

When we went to visit my grandparents, Nana would bring out a stack of newspaper clippings of cartoon drawings she had collected for all her grandchildren, to entertain us quietly. We would look for and find a little character called *Wally*. I recall, when I used to visit her, she would make a stew with rice mixed together, which she would call *carna* and would feed my cousins and I one mouth at a time with her hands while we searched for Wally in the cartoon pictures.

The living room was where visitors were entertained, so all the grandchildren had to be respectful of everything that was in or that entered their living room. Grandpa taught me how to play "Chopsticks" on the piano and would practice it with me often. On one occasion, when I was alone with him in the living room, which was exceedingly rare, I said, "Grandpa, can you play and sing me *'Danny Boy,'* please?"

"Charm, we don't have long, just one more, as dinner will be ready soon."

He got up from the piano stool and shut the living room door. I was sitting on the sofa, waiting for him to play me another tune. While sitting back on the stool, facing the piano, he beckoned to me to go over to him, so I stood up and walked over to his right side. As I stood there, he said softly while playing a tune on the piano,

"I know you can see people that others can't. Charm, I see your orbs too. What are their names?"

"Venus and Maximillian. I call them V and Max. You see them too, Grandpa?"

"Yes, Charm. Hello, Max and Venus."

"Just call her V Grandpa!"

"Oh sorry, V. Please listen carefully, all of you. We don't have long. Someone will come in. I am unsure whether you know this or not but there is an entity that we call Reaper. He is dark in colour and about the size of a football. He can be any shape and is generally high up on the back area of a person's body. He has been feeding off our family for generations."

"Yes, Grandpa, they know about him."

"Wait, wait, don't say anything, just listen, please."

Line needs to be removed but I don't know how!

I nodded and Grandpa played on.

"A curse, as you'll know, was put upon our family many centuries ago. Reaper is not his real name. No one knows his real one. If they did, then he could be banished. He jumps from person to person and has the ability to not just feed off fear but to enter a person and make them do things. He causes them to be angry or sad and bad things happen. He causes chaos and illnesses in that person and that person does things that they wouldn't normally do. Watch out for this energy, please. Protect my granddaughter. Charm, you pray, especially when you see him so that he stays away from you and your family."

"What type of things does Reaper do Grandpa?"

"Sicknesses. He can make a person very unwell

Nana opened and popped her head in around the door and told us our food was ready and our conversation ended there. I loved my grandpa dearly and when he passed away, it really affected me deeply. He would play the tune on his piano and sing *'Danny Boy'* to me beautifully. I really do miss him. I know I will see him again and on that day, I hope we have a huge celebration. A family reunion, just like we did when I was young.

"Danny Boy" – GENTRI Covers (Lyrics)

"The only way that we can live is if we grow.
The only way we can grow is if we change.
The only way we can change is if we learn.
The only way we can learn is if we are exposed.
And the only way that we are exposed is if we
throw ourselves into the open"

C. Joybell

My Parents

My Dad and My Mom

Chapter 6

Early School Years

My parents worked extremely hard to support my brother, sister and me. Queens Park train station, buses and *Salisbury Junior Mix School* were at the bottom of our street, within walking distance. We passed shops and our local church as we walked to school. I can't remember exactly when Dad bought a car but I know it was while we were living at that house.

***

My first day at school was traumatic for me. While I clung hold of my Mom at the school gate, I told her I would call the police if she left me there alone. Weeks went by and every day I would make such a fuss that the teachers would ask my brother Tony to be with me. He would sit in my classroom until I'd calmed down. Friends were in short supply by the middle of the year. Some of the kids knew I openly had conversations with people they could not see. They were cruel and teased me all the time, taunting, "Charm has an imaginary friend."

One girl was okay though. She also heard her guardian; her name was Sandi. She was a foster child. She was the one who advised me not to talk to Max or V if anyone was around. One day Sandi was sick and didn't go into school. V, I suppose sensed I was feeling lost and insecure, said to me, "Sweetheart, drawing and colouring would be something you'll enjoy doing alone on days like this one. Charm, try hopscotch or your skipping rope," she suggested.

V's suggestions were always spot on. She knew me so well, and amazingly, they all worked! Sadly, by the end of that first school year, the voice of Sandi's guardian got fainter and fainter and then, she couldn't hear him anymore. One day Sandi also just disappeared. I was told she went to stay with her new Mom and Dad. Max reassuringly told me, "Charm, this type of thing happens to many kids. It's normal but, my girl, it won't happen to us." I knew I was different from the other kids. Unfortunately, this only added to the frustration and isolation I felt, which always seemed to rise like a huge wave, around break and lunchtimes at school.

"No One" – Alicia Keys (Lyrics)

Chapter 7

Bonfire

*I*t was 5 November, bonfire night party in 1975, when my Aunt Jane and Uncle Gary invited us to their house for dinner to sit around the communal bonfire and watch the fireworks. They had three children at this time: My eldest cousin Gary Jr., who we nicknamed Gaz, was fourteen; Leanne, Lea, was twelve; and Simon, Si, ten years old. They lived on a government-owned counsel estate called Coppermead Close in Cricklewood, Kilburn.

Gaz, an extremely handsome and muscular teen, like the rest of his family, had dark brown hair and light brown eyes, with a tanned complexion. He was always smiling and joyful, energy-filled, intelligent, kind and hilariously funny. Every word that came out of his mouth was entertaining and he was a delight to be around.

My cousin Si and my brother Tony were the same age. I was a year younger, nine. Tony and Si were the best of friends, always running around together and playing football in the park close by. When our families met up in Kilburn, Tony and Si, as usual, ran off to play in the park. Si was fit and thin. Like his brother, he had cracking good looks and when he smiled, which was often, he had a dimple on his right cheek. Si was even-tempered, a happy-go-lucky boy who was always neat and clean, a real go-getter, sociable and clever.

As Mom and Dad would always arrive early, we were the first guests who showed up at Auntie Jane and Uncle Gary's house. All the adults would sit together around the dining room table, chatting, drinking and smoking cigarettes. Terry, my baby sister, was five years old and would rather read her books than play. She was placed on the sofa and was quite comfortable there with her Ladybird and Aesop Fables books, crayons, and colouring books.

On this particular day, Lea and I sat chatting on the park bench outside about the problems I had at school with the female bullies. She would give me advice on how to deal with the troublemakers, which was reassuring.

"Punch 'em in the face. They'll soon leave you alone!" was her usual response.

Lea knew about Max and V. She would ask questions to them. They would answer her through me, of course. On that day, she asked Max, "Was I born before?"

***

"Yes, many times," Max replied and continued, "Once you were accused of being a witch, just like my Charm girl. She knows this and I've mentioned it to her before. During the Civil War in 1645, both of you were sisters. Then you lived together in a village with your families in East Anglia. You'd collect certain herbs, leaves, flowers, bark and plants and would make home remedies to sell. These remedies would combat illnesses and complaints to do with the body. It's medicine!

"You were phenomenally successful at healing people and learned this from your grandmother and mother. Girl, I'm telling you, this art was passed down from generation to generation. They got it all wrong as there wasn't anything witchiness involved in it. It was a talent. There was no brewing or chanting or anything like that.

"People still do this today to make medicines. Anyway, sorry to tell you this but you were both taken, had trials and were drowned, one after the other. In the end, you were both found guilty of witchcraft as both bodies floated in the water when released from the ropes. Don't worry, Lea, your descendants are still alive today and your recipes are still used. Some are called old wives' tales, some are lost to history but just for now," Max replied.

***

Lea was amazing, like a wise big sister, doting and protective of me and my cousin Jen, who was three months older than me. Lea was slightly taller than Gaz and her classmates at school. She was not intimidating to the other girls in her class. She gave them no reason to be. They were jealous of her looks as the boys would swarm around her, like bees buzzing around their hive. She was one of the most popular girls at her school—the queen bee, streetwise, strong-willed and blunt.

Empowered by her good looks, compared with all the other girls, she was untouchable and stunningly beautiful, looking more like sixteen than twelve, with an hour-glass figure, long thick flowing locks that would reach down to her waist, if not tied in a high ponytail. Like me, Lea was not allowed to wear makeup and wore clothes suitable for her age, dresses, skirts and T-shirts. However, I can say even a sackcloth would look great on her.

While sitting on the bench waiting for it to get darker and impatient for our other cousin, Jen, to arrive, Lea suggested we stroll along the path to the other side of the park, to an area enclosed by a large, wired fence with stadium floodlights that oversaw a manicured football field. As we approached the fence, we were quite surprised when the automatic lights went out as it became darker instantly. Lea sparked up a cigarette.

"Try it, it's not that bad," Lea said, handing me one.

We heard Jen calling our names and could see her running up to us in the dim light.

"Oh, my god, what ya got there? Got a fag spare, Lea?" Jen said.

"Here, you can have mine. I don't think that I will like it," I said, handing Jen the cigarette quickly.

"Thanks, Charm, we'll share it. This brand's not bad, B & H," Jen said.

She puffed on it, trying to light it off Lea's cigarette. Once lit, she took a huge drag in, held her breath and handed the cigarette back to me. Between the two fingers of my right hand, I grasped it like a pair of tweezers, near the butt, put it to my lips and I dragged on it ever so slightly and breathed the smoke into my lungs a little, then blew it right back out again quickly.

"That's Benson & Hedges . . . "Here, look," Lea said as she pulled out a box from her dress pocket, a gold packet of cigarettes.

"You can get these in 10s and 20s but I usually buy a few fags from our sweet shop down the road. They sell them individually and I restock 'em in here. It's handy, this small box of ten's are compact and easy to hide" Lea said.

"It's all right . . . You're right . . . It's quite nice," I said surprised while dragging on the cigarette, slowly taking the smoke deeper and deeper into my lungs each time.

It burned going down my throat. I enjoyed it. We passed it back and forth between Jen and I until we finished the fag. We headed back to the bench. I asked Lea for a few extra *Tic-Tacs* to pop into my mouth to take away the smell of smoke on my breath. We strolled and chatted about everything young girls talked about; the boys that we fancied, our troubles, the latest music that we liked and what we got up to since we last saw each other!

As we walked, passing us by was a large family of people carrying many items: a dirty stained mattress, a coffee table and other wooden pieces of furniture. We watched laughing as men tried stacking them on top of and around the enormous pile of wood and junk, which stood over six feet tall with a single bed's wooden frame perched up high, resembling a cherry on top of a cake, in the middle of the park.

It was like a huge trash heap with everything burnable, all muddled together and piled higher and higher on top. The mattress, they decided to leave near the bottom, leaning upright, shoved in between a broken wardrobe and a chest of draws, both projecting out of the mountain. The mattress then had some stability.

Our parents came outside with Aunties, kitchen chairs and some snacks. They set up near the park bench before it got too dark, to see eight men spraying then lighting the heap. Lea and I greeted Auntie Edna and Uncle Adam with a hello and a kiss on the cheek each. All the kids in our family were brought up to greet elders, Aunts, Uncles and their friends. It is tradition and out of respect to call the elders, Auntie or Uncle too.

The bonfire was much higher now. It was lit and with sparklers in our hands, we all watched Catharine wheels spin on posts and rockets go off randomly in the distance every now and again. It was supposed to be a joyous occasion but for some reason, I had a strange feeling come over me, a feeling of dread.

I heard a familiar voice, whispering. "Today is the day when Si will die. Tony will start a lifelong journey in and out of hospital to treat burns, and for reconstructive surgeries on his face," Max said.

"Why will Si die? And what does reconstructive surgeries mean?" I asked Max telepathically.

"Charm, you can change this, this is not in their life's plan. Evil is here. Call them. They are in danger near the fire. GO NOW!" He didn't answer either of my questions. Instead, he showed me!

***

In a flash, I had a vision of Si buried underneath a wooden bedframe. I could see him covered in flames through the struts of the wooden frame, where a mattress would be. He was pinned down and wasn't moving. Tony was using his whole strength trying to get the frame off Si. The entire front of his body was burning. His skin and flesh seemed to melt off him. His clothes were in flames.

***

I was with Jen and Lea. They were shocked when I dropped my lit sparker on the grass. I started sprinting towards the bonfire, screaming frantically.

"Si, Si, Tony, where are you? Anthony, Simon, answer me!"

"Yes, we're here," they called back.

Looking up, I could see the head side of the bedframe perched burning on the top of the heap. I could hear their voices on the other side of the bonfire, near the mattress.

"Move away, that way, away from the fire!" I shouted, hoping they could see me waving my arms and screaming louder as I approached the mattress.

In that Moment, I couldn't see them. It was getting darker, and I realised everything was distorted by the flickering of the fire. It was difficult to recognise people's faces but seconds later, I saw Si first, picking up sticks, then noticed Tony close to him, talking to some other boys. They were about twenty feet away from me.

"Move away from the fire, away from here!" I said, screaming frantically, flapping my arms from my chest forwards, directing them towards the crowd on the far outskirts of the unmarked perimeter around the bonfire.

I was swimming, doing breast strokes in the cold dimmed night air. All the boys dropped their sticks. They turned on their heels and bolted towards the crowd, looking in amazement; wondering what was wrong with me.

Within seconds, right in front of me, exactly where Si had been standing, tumbled the bedframe. It fell together with an avalanche of burning debris, which made me jump backwards in quick response. I could see my Dad running towards me. He scooped me up in his arms and carried me back to the park bench, where the adults and my little sister had gathered. Lea and Jen came running up to us with fizzled sparklers in their hands. Si and Tony sprinted towards us too.

"Thanks, Max. Thank you so much. How did you know?" I thought.

At first, everyone was more concerned about what was going on with me, instead of looking out for the fireworks that sometimes zipped across the sky. By the time Gaz came, my cousins and our families were all together at the park bench and the Coppermead community fireworks started. It was a spectacular display of explosions in the sky and an incredibly lucky escape for Si and Tony, thanks to Max. My five cousins and I were awfully close. We discussed the near-miss and agreed it was a lucky escape.

"You must be a witch or something," Si remarked.

"Once maybe but not in this lifetime," I replied.

"He Ain't Heavy, He's My Brother" – The Hollies (Lyrics)

"A house is made of brick and mortar, but home is made by the people who live there"

M.K. Soni

Chapter 8

The House on Springfield Gardens

As time went by and we three kids grew, our living accommodation became cramped. Mom and Dad moved us all into a council house in Kingsbury on Springfield Gardens. There, I started at *Oliver Goldsmith Elementary School*. By then, I was addicted to cigarettes and often stole them from my parents. My psychic abilities had progressed. I was able to see earthbound spirits and that house was occupied by three spirits. V, my guardian, did a good job keeping me safe and I was only scared on a few occasions while living there.

"No problem, Charm, I can handle them," she used to say confidently with her gentle voice.

***

My Mom, who is also sensitive to the people who have died, was the first person in our family to experience the spirits in the council house. It happened on the first day she entered the house on Springfield Gardens in Kingsbury. She had picked up the keys from the Brent councilman, who is a government landlord, and together with my Auntie Veronica, my grandmother's sister, set out early to preview the house.

They went by bus and had to climb up a steep hill and pass Oliver Goldsmith Elementary School. By the time they got to the front door, they were out of breath. The house was two-story; it had a long, wide shared driveway to the left, leading to two detached garages and a gate to enter the backyard of the council property.

Mom used the key to unlock the front glass door. She pulled down on the latch and they both entered the house with little effort. The house was vacant. It was an open plan. Wooden *Parka floors* were throughout the living room, dining room and galley kitchen areas. In the living room was a huge bay window and at the back of the house were double doors leading into a white tiled room I call the sunroom, which was a mostly glass, conservatory/covered patio. Beyond that was the backyard.

The front door was directly in front of the steps. The steps and upstairs were carpeted; at the top of the stairs on the left wall was a large glass window. There were three bedrooms and a bathroom on the upper floor. The master had a bed in it; on the bed was a large cardboard box with new fabric, curtains and equipment to make and design lampshades.

Mom and Auntie immediately noticed that all over the carpet, on the bed and scattered all around the room were small brass-coloured hooks and eyes. These curtain hooks were used to attach the curtain to the curtain rod. The strewn brass pieces were too numerous to count. It was a very unusual sight. They started picking them up and putting them in the box but did not complete collecting them all because there were too many.

The room was bright, thick beige drapes hung, drawn back and gathered either side of the huge bay window that overlooked Springfield Gardens. Plain white net curtains were still hanging up too, obviously one of the last things to be taken down, and still to be packed by the previous tenant. On the opposite wall facing the bed, were wall-to-wall fitted cream-coloured bedroom hanging closets, shelves and storage cupboards, from the ceiling to the floor. It also had a large mirror nestled in the middle with a glass shelf underneath. Brass hooks and eyes were all over that too.

They left that room, closed the door and entered the bathroom. It was quite small and had a white porcelain toilet, pedestal wash basin and bathtub. An amazingly simple design but clean. It had a fairly large window in the room, which let in a lot of light; the driveway was below to the left of the house. One of the bedrooms was a small box room. It was next to the master bedroom and also faced the front of the house. This room had nothing at all in it. The window was long and narrow and had no curtains.

The last room upstairs was fairly big, about the size of the master. It had full-length fitted white wall units, shelves, a desk area and cupboards along two of the largest walls. A huge flat window viewed scenes of the backyard, the detached garage, and the sloped roof of the sunroom's extension below. While inspecting the closets, Auntie had discovered that one of them with double doors had a hideaway, collapsible, pull-down, single bed. They both loved the house and were heading downstairs to look at the kitchen and sunroom when they heard the toilet flushing.

They both went back into the bathroom. Nobody was in there. The toilet's tank was still filling with water. They thought it was weird but carried on viewing the house. The kitchen was galley style. It was clean and it had a convenient little opening over the countertop to pass meals through into the dining room. The kitchen had a large window with three smaller windows over it. It had two doors, one on each end. One leading into the living and dining room and the other into the sunroom.

The sunroom was full of windows. It was quite big with long built-in benches that had removable soft-top white seats below the windows. One bench was open. They could see it full of printed business cards, large unopened packets of unused lined index cards, and other papers. A little empty blue children's tent was erected on the tiled floor. In that room, there was a locked door leading out into the garden.

A short while later, they were ready to leave. When they tried to open the front door, it would not open. There was nowhere to unlock the door with a key from the inside of the house, so Mom and Auntie called out to a neighbor gardening across the street. Mom opened the tiny window in the kitchen and gave him the key to unlock the door from the outside. He couldn't. Mom and Auntie tried all the doors and windows inside the house. They were all locked.

They were trapped in there all morning. They flagged down some schoolchildren on their lunch break from the elementary school, who brought back their principal to try the key and unlatch the door. He tried with no avail but he promised to call the council. Meanwhile, passersby and other neighbors were all unsuccessful too. As far as the crowd were concerned, the door was already unlocked. It should open!

Debates were flying as to what could be holding the door shut: the bolt, the latch, a crooked frame. The old lady next door was passing Mom and Auntie a cup of tea through the window, when the councilman pulled up outside the house. He turned the key, unlatched the door and it opened easily.

Everyone stood around in disbelief when the man said, "Opening a door is a simple thing to do. This is a total waste of my time!"

Auntie's face went red, her lips tightened. This once quiet mild-mannered elderly woman burst outside. She pushed past the councilman and frantically started sparking her lighter, then with her cigarette flapping between her fingertips, as she wagged her bony finger in the man's face, she screamed.

"How dare you suggest we are incompetent, young man? You should be ashamed of yourself!"

The man, shocked with her reaction, left swiftly, leaving the crowd. Mom and Auntie were terribly upset. They were getting late to pick us up from school. They had two other choices of council houses to view but decided to wait to do that another day. It ended up that both houses were in bad condition and were in bad parts of

London. Even though Mom knew something was not right about the Springfield Gardens house, she did not feel unsafe, so she told Dad she liked that one the best and we moved in shortly after.

One of Dad's first chores were to change the front door lock; he also took out the folding bed in the second bedroom. Replacing it with a bunk bed so my sister Theresa and I could share a room. Anthony's room was a little cramped. He liked having his own space. We all enjoyed living in that house.

I liked our bedroom and used to sit on the top bunk. There, I'd write down the correct song lyrics, from the tunes I listen to on my radio. It was easier to remember the lyrics that way. Songs like *'Benny and the Jets,'* written by *Bernie Taupin* and sung by the amazing *'Sir Elton John'* that was first released in 1974, was played often on the radio. It was impossible for me to get those lyrics exactly correct, it was a challenge, as Max, V and I loved that song and wanted it in my collection of music lyrics cards!

I couldn't believe my luck that I found those index cards and claimed them all mine, announcing to my siblings, *'Finders Keepers.'* We all knew that the person who said those words first, got to keep the cards. It was rare that I won; I was chuffed! They were 12.7cm by 7.6cm, a nice size. Each packet was identical, white with one hundred lined cards in them. I found two thousand cards all together in absolutely perfect condition. They were ideal for song lyrics to be filed alphabetically for quick reference when the weekly Top 40 music hits were played.

I would also draw pictures on them or use my sketch book with oil pastels and coloured pencils that I got as a gift for Christmas. I would talk to *The Lady in White* who used to visit me often in that room. As I drew, she told me she lived next door and would walk through the wall, come out of Mom's closet then walk through my parents' wall into mine. She was really nice. Max and V liked her also.

Two other earthbound spirits would often come to that house: *The Grey Army Man* and the person who was always in a pink flowered dress, whom I named *The Ghost Girl*. Her name was

Mary. Mom had told me the story of being trapped in the house when I was a lot older and we'd already moved out by then, so I never found out why the spirits wanted to keep her and Auntie Veronica in the house that day.

"Green, Green Grass of Home" – Tom Jones (Lyrics)

My Purple Suit

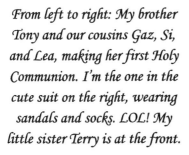

From left to right: My brother Tony and our cousins Gaz, Si, and Lea, making her first Holy Communion. I'm the one in the cute suit on the right, wearing sandals and socks. LOL! My little sister Terry is at the front.

My Mom; little sister Terry, two years old; brother Tony, seven years old; and me, six years old, in my favorite purple suit.

"The first to apologise is the bravest.
The first to forgive is the strongest.
The first to forget is the happiest."

Unknown

Chapter 9

Three Spirits

One night, when my sister Terry woke up, she saw a large brownish shadow, close up, by the side of the bunk bed, looking at me while I slept. She was so scared and ran into my parents' bedroom and left me sleeping alone. She told us the next morning what she had seen.

I would call him The Grey Army Man because when I used to see him, his face was greyish brown. He didn't look healthy. He was clean-shaven, had a neat mustache, side-parted brown hair and little sideburns. His eyes were hazel brown with a slim drawn face. He had a lovely smile. I caught him many times in my bedroom when I rolled over to change positions in bed and asked him each time to "Please leave me alone!"

He wore a khaki cotton uniform. The shirt had two large flap pockets, one on either side of his chest. His top button was open. It had short sleeves to the elbows. He had a light-coloured belt around his waist. His khaki shorts was down to his knees. He had long cream-coloured socks and ankle-high brown boots. His cap matched the colour of his clothes and perched on an angle, more towards the right of his head. V said once, "He's okay. He was just visiting you from the light to see how you are."

Max said he was a family member who died in World War 2; his name is Bobby. My Dad's brother was named Bobby. I recall my Mom telling me Uncle Bobby had died many years before I was born and that he died in that war. I didn't meet very many members of my Dad's side of the family. If I had a photo of Uncle Bobby in his uniform, then I'm 100% sure I could have confirmed if it were him.

***

Another person was a young girl, around twelve. She was always dressed in a pink flowered dress. She would go around the downstairs of the house on Springfield Gardens, looking for something. I'd call her *The Ghost Girl*. She did not know she was dead. She had no clue we were living there. She bothered no one. The Ghost Girl walked through our furniture and walls; she did not say a word. A few times I asked her if she would like some help to find what she'd lost. She would ignore me and walk the same path through our house and do the same thing every night, like she was stuck in a loop.

Max said, "Her name is Mary. She's now like a memory of the past, imprinted within the house. Once, she did reside around here."

V said I didn't need protection from Mary, The Ghost Girl, as she doesn't know I was around.

***

Anthony and I started *Oliver Goldsmith School*, about a five-minute walk from the house. Dad was still working at night and slept most of the day. He made sure he spent some time with us each evening before leaving for work. On his days off, when I came in from school, Dad would make me tea and buttered toast and we would sit and watch *Harold Lloyd, Tarzan* and other black-and-white programs on the TV, until Mom came home from working in the West End of London.

Mom would tuck me in at night, say prayers, kiss me and leave me to sleep. She would do the same for Anthony then would spend time with Theresa, bathing her and reading *Aesop fables* and *Ladybird* books in her room, which was next to mine. I would drift off to sleep after praying with Max and V while listening to Mom read about *'The Quack Toad,' 'The Fox Without A Tail,' 'The Mischievous Dog',* and all the other characters that dwell within the collection of those books. Mom saved up and bought them weekly for little Terry.

***

It was around this time when I started to feel pain in my face, just under my ears. Mom took me to the doctor. He checked me for an ear infection and he also checked my throat. I had enlarged tonsils and he thought it could be tonsilitis or mumps. A few days later, I was in pain again and the right side of my face, just under my ear, became very swollen. I was back at the doctor's repeatedly. I couldn't fake the swelling and they knew something was not right. The doctor referred me to the dentist.

For quite some time, the dentist filled all my grinders, but nothing helped. A few years later, I was still feeling pain, and everything he did didn't make the pain any better. It was reported in the newspaper that the dentist was a crook, filling children's teeth for extra money regardless of whether they needed to be repaired or not. So, I was taken back to the doctor again many times for swelling and excruciating face pain.

***

I not only had swelling in my face that occasionally occurred that no one knew how to cure but tonsilitis was a huge problem for me too. One day in mid-November, I was extremely ill, at home, from school with a high fever. My Dad was looking after me in the living room. Dad said to me, if I go to sleep for a while, he will make the

Christmas season start early. I slept peacefully for a few hours. When I woke up, my Dad surprised me: He put up the Christmas tree and decorated it.

He decided to do something different that year and hung many colourful Christmas baubles and lightweight tree ornaments dotted all over the ceiling in the living room and dining room with pushpins. The decorations were all in different shapes and sizes and were hung at different lengths with sewing thread. It sounds awful, but it was lovely. We had many tree decorations we never really used but that year he used every last one. The ceilings matched the tree!

***

When I was older, Mom told me of another story that happened one night. It was around the time when Dad had decorated the ceilings downstairs. The incident transpired while she and my sister were in Mom's bedroom reading, which she did nightly. She heard a male voice calling her name clearly, two or three times, and the voice was coming from downstairs. Mom said she was frightened and waited up as Theresa slept in her bed that night, until Dad came home in the early parts of the morning. I wondered if it was Uncle Bobby or we had more than three spirits within that house, others that I didn't know about and hadn't met yet.

"Sound of Silence" – Simon & Garfunkel (Lyrics)

Chapter 10

The Dog Alleyway

*A*round the first year of *Oliver Goldsmith school* (Olly Golly), I met Neena (Nee). She was instantly my best friend. Nee and I would always play together. I knew I liked her from the second we met; she was outgoing and spoke up for me and for herself with the bullies at our school. Marisha (Mari) and I met a year or so later. She had moved into a house a few doors away from mine on Springfield Gardens.

I had seen her a few times at school, in the playground by herself. On a Friday after school, I recall inviting her to play with the neighborhood kids and me on our street. She accepted immediately and we had a lot of fun together that weekend, playing knock down ginger, skipping rope and hopscotch. The very next day, when I saw Nee at school, I introduced Mari to her; we all got on so well. It was as if we had all known one another for years.

Mari became my second-best friend from that day on. We three went through elementary school together; they made some great memories for me. We ended up going to junior high together at *Kingsbury High School* and asked our parents if we could walk to school together. Surprisingly, they all said, "Yes!"

***

I got into a routine pretty quickly. On a normal school morning, I'd wake up, take a shower, dress into my school uniform, sneak my makeup and put books and homework into my school bag, then leave home extra early and walk to Mari's house with breakfast in my hand, which was usually a banana, a slice of toast or something like that. When I got to Mari's house, her Mom would usually be altering her school tie, brushing her hair and styling it into braids or a ponytail. She'd always be rushing her Mom, pleading with her to hurry up, so we could go to pick up Nee.

When we walked out of sight from her house, Mari, in a matter of seconds, would remove the clips, bands and grips her Mom painstakingly put on. I would have killed to have her hair. It was thick, black, long, flowing and shiny. Mine, on the other hand, was shoulder-length, curly and unmanageable. It flicked up in every direction and whatever I did to it, it still looked terrible.

Marisha had a fantastic personality: caring, quiet and gentle. She loved animals, especially dogs. She longed to have one. She was attractive, thin, with brown eyes, lovely shaped black eyebrows and extra-long thick black eyelashes, which complimented her clear tanned complexion. Mari always had a smile on her face. Her constant giggle was contagious and nothing ever got her down, except for the bullies in school that harassed us. She could draw *Snoopy* blindfolded and loved the *Charlie Brown* characters. They were sketched all over her school homework folders and book covers in different poses. I don't ever recall arguing with her.

Mari and I would have to walk through the dog alleyway, which was a shortcut to pick up Nee. She lived a brisk 15-minute walk from our street and we'd have to back track a bit from Nee's house to get to school which was another 30-minute walk away but we didn't mind as long as we were together. When we got there, we'd run up her stairs and lock her bedroom door, then combine and lay out neatly all our makeup, which we produced from out of our backpacks, onto Nee's bed, and each of us would choose which colour lipstick, eye shadow and blusher to wear that day. We'd style and straighten our hair, shave our legs and give one another fashion tips and talk about the songs we liked on the radio before leaving for school each morning, continuing our conversations on our journey there.

Neena was also attractively tanned. Her long dark brown hair was absolutely straight; she always styled it with a side parting and a cute little fringe swept delicately over her eyebrows. Her hair cascaded down her back on top of her uniform, touching her slim curved hips. Nee always wore black rubber bands on her wrist, just in case she had to whip her hair up at school.

She had a slim pretty face, gorgeous dark brown eyes and thin pinkish lips; her body was elegantly shaped. Nee was a straight-shooter and confident. Even though she was afraid of dogs, she was brave and strong-willed. She was uniquely comical, cracking jokes at every chance she could get. Her determination and loyalty to her friends and family is what attracted me to her.

***

Mari and I would walk through the dog alleyway together to and from school. On our way home from school, just off Wakemans Hill Road, there is a road we had to turn down. At the bottom of that short road was the dog alley but a few houses in, on the left-hand side was where the German shepherd dogs used to live, two or three of them, all chained up outside in the front yard of this short-gated house.

We would call out loudly at the top of the road and peek onto the street, just in case one of the dogs got loose. Everyone who regularly went down that road called out from Wakemans Hill or from the other direction before coming out of the alley! The dogs would bark, lunge, snarl and growl every time anyone walked by. It must have been extremely irritating for the neighbors in that area.

It was important to Nee for us to shout aloud at the dogs to and from school. She was chased and bitten by one of those dogs, which had escaped from its chains from the gated house, when she walked by it once. She had to get a tetanus shot and a huge bandage was wrapped around her leg for days. She limped around for weeks and still has the scar.

If Mari were sick, which was not that often, I'd walk to Nee's house on The Ridgeway by myself. I hated going through the dog alleyway alone. I was used to the spirit that I would hear screaming at us from somewhere in the tree-filled and unkept bushy area. It still scared me. I had an uncomfortable feeling about that place but when Mari walked beside me, it wasn't that bad. We'd just walk on the path through the trees on each side, chatting and laughing. Mari had no clue what I was hearing. I wasn't going to tell her. She'd think I was a crazy freak! I didn't want to lose her or Nee as friends.

***

Once, I did tell them a story that had happened to my Auntie Helen and they were so scared. After that, I kept my mouth shut about supernatural and paranormal stuff. I recall the last time I walked through that alley by myself. I was thirteen. It was a time when Mari was sick and was unable to go to school. I knew I had to sprint through the alley because Max had told me many years prior three spirits were there.

"A long time ago, one woman was raped and murdered there. Charm girl, that's the one you call *'The Screaming Woman'* and there are two men that dwell there also. None of them know that they have died. Hoo-wee! One of the men died from an accidental drug overdose and the other was a homeless man. He died naturally in the alley while sleeping under one of those trees. It is important that you are relaxed and calm when going through because they can sense that you hear them."

As I approached the dog alleyway, I prepared myself to sprint, just as I did a few times before when alone. This time was different.

I was nervous and scared, not just because of the spirits but because of the vicious dogs too. Suddenly, an overwhelming sensation of fear and dread rushed over me as I started to run, and while in mid-stride, the unexpected happened. I saw a full-bodied apparition of a spirit lady. I stopped still on the path in the middle of the alley.

The lady looked like she was in her early twenties. At first, she was about fifteen feet away from me, bleeding from the nose and she had cuts that bled on her forehead to her temple. Then in the blink of an eye, she appeared, right up in my face, whispering desperately, "Help me, please. Help me . . . He's coming. Please," she said with a panicked shaky voice.

I could feel her fear and hear distress in her voice. Tears were streaming from her blue eyes down her dirty thin face, which left streak marks where tears once fell. Her red lipstick smudged from her quivering lips to her left cheek. She was Caucasian, with shoulder-length thinning beach blond hair, which was very messy with a few little dead leaves entangled in it.

Turning her head, a little to look behind her then snapping her head quickly to look back at me, she bent down to whisper in my ear while she put her dirty hands on my shoulders.

"Please, please! I'll do anything. Keep me safe, please!"

She pointed behind her. Her fingernails had red nail polish but was mostly caked in dirt and mud up to the cuticles. Her knee-length cream dress was also very dirty.

"He's coming. Let's go—let's go now."

She was visibly trembling. I could see someone standing in the trees behind her. I gasped and she ran behind me, using me as a shield. I was petrified and stood watching this man.

"You shouldn't be here. Get out of here. What are you doing on my land?" The Shabby Man acted as if he was drunk, swaying and slurring his words.

He was Caucasian and looked filthy and unshaven. He had dirty, dusty brown pants and an off-grey shirt on, messy longish greasy hair, tatty brown shoes and was wearing a shabby, dirty long brown coat. When the man walked towards us, V said in a gentle voice, "It's all right, Charm, you are not in danger. They can't hurt you. He's a lost soul. Can you talk to them?"

"No bloody way," I said under my breath.

I turned towards The Lady but she evaporated in front of me. I looked back and the shabby, unshaven, scruffy guy had gone too. I was about to run in his direction towards Nee's house, when another bloke appeared on the pathway, blocking my exit. I could hear the dogs barking and howling behind him.

He didn't look well. He was pale, about 6-foot-something tall and had a blank look on his face, with his mouth slightly open and his jaw a little dropped. He mouthed something but no words came out. I don't know what he said. He wore a lime green T-shirt and black jogging pants.

This lanky-looking man stood there staring at me. Around his eyes were black circles that stood out prominently on his light-coloured skin. He was holding something in his right hand that looked like a syringe. I could see the needle as it glinted in the sunlight. Around the bicep of his left arm dangled a piece of rubber attached to a brown band on his left arm and tight over his T-shirt sleeve.

"Help him, Charm, sweetheart, just talk to him," V said.

I didn't. Instead, I spun on my heals and scurried out of there as quickly as I could. I ran through a smaller alley back onto Springfield Gardens, past Mari's house, back to my own home. With my heart still pounding and still out of breath, I called my Mom at work.

"Hi, Mom."

"Hi. What are you doing at home, Charm? You'll be late," she said.

"I'm not feeling well today. I'm feeling sick. I think I'm going to throw up. I must have what Mari's got. She's not going to school today. Is it okay if I go back to bed and have a day off?" I said, genuinely wheezing and about to spew.

"You don't sound good at all. Go to bed . . ." She was saying something else as I flung the phone down.

I rushed to the bathroom, just managing to reach the toilet, and threw up. The phone rang, stopped ringing, then rang again but I still had my head in the toilet. I did call Mom back and apologized for hanging up on her then went to my bedroom and cuddled Hector for a while as Max and V comforted me. They were floating in orb shapes above my toes as I lay with my beloved teddy on my bed.

"This is the reason you were born, to help lost souls and spirits go into the light. You're here to bring comfort to their loved ones and to act as a medium between dimensions," Max said.

"Nope!" I said bluntly and continued, "Nope, no bloody way!"

"Sweetheart, we know this is difficult for you and that you are scared of spirits sometimes. Those ones couldn't hurt you, and anyway, I'm here to protect you. Max can too and will warn and guide you."

"I'm not talking to no creepy ghosts, V, got it? It isn't going to happen," I replied, pushing Hector's back up against my face, and mumbling through the bear, I continued, "I don't mind the nice ones but the scary ones all covered in blood, no, no way . . . Just leave me alone, guys, I just can't talk right now!"

***

From that day on, if Mari were not walking to pick up Nee with me, I would wake up extra, extra early and walk the long way around to get to Nee's house on time or if I'm running late, I'll call and ask her to meet me at Kingsbury High School.

"You've Got a Friend" – Carole King (Lyrics)

The Dog Alleyway

This is a photo of the tree, under which 'The Shabby Man' died and where he first stood, when he first appeared to me in 'The Dog Alleyway.'

Taken in 2022 in 'The Dog Alleyway' U.K.

*"The greatest glory in living
lies not in never falling,
but in rising every time we fall."*

Nelson Mandela

Chapter 11

Where Your Book Begins

*W*ith some persuasion and after Max and V agreed to answer some questions, eventually, I relented and decided to find out some more about life and death in general, and to ask the niggling questions I was curious about.

I've known from a young age, through playing charades and games with Max, how to figure out what spirits were trying to say to me, signs and symbols to interpret messages they had for me. I needed to be sure before I agreed to work with Max and V to save souls. They wanted me to write a book and told me multiple times, the things to put into it about the afterlife. I wrote down many notes, even so, this book was difficult for me to write.

Here are just a few questions I had asked throughout my childhood but unfortunately, I didn't write down who said what when answering some of my questions. They were all answered by either Max or V; if unsure, I have left those ones blank to who spoke.

(*Here are some of my notes*).

"Start from the beginning, guys. Who decides when we are born and why are some babies born sick?"

Max said, "God chooses our date of birth, exactly where we are born and our date of death. We all are informed in advance if we would be born with a birth defect or an illness by The Elder Guides, who are part of *The Council of Elders* that answer directly to God."

"When will this be decided?" I asked.

"*The Delegation of Extra Challenges* will occur during the meetings with The Elder Guides when we are in heaven. This is in addition to the challenges we have chosen for ourselves. We all know our group's mission too and what we want to learn and achieve in our own individual lifetimes."

"What about miscarried and very young children? Why do they have to die?" I asked.

"Before the child is sent back, they already know if they will have a short life. Some other examples of a short life: To die due to a miscarriage. Or sweetheart, they would know if they will be born with a health problem at birth, that will result in an early death. In this scenario, the child will know if their last Moments on earth is in a crib or cot. They will know if they will be alone, without another living person with them, or who will be with them at the Moment of their death, for an easier crossing over transition."

"How do you prepare a soul to go through this?"

"After we are told these things, we will be schooled beforehand so that we know what to expect and can live through the Moment relatively unafraid. The plans made for those life scenarios, are faultless."

"What about for the people who are murdered?"

"Sometimes people choose to be murdered, just for the knowledge and experience of going through the event. This death is controlled and planned extensively with all participants that will be involved. This is different to if a person was murdered by another person's free will. Which is not a pre-planned act and is a sin for the murderer. The person who was murdered will eventually go to heaven after a period of learning and rest. Usually, they will be on the same level as they were before. The murderer will face judgement for this sin, at the time of their death"

"What happens to the babies that die?"

"Some of the people in our group may choose to be souls who die in the womb, as a miscarried child of fellow soul group members who are living life on earth. It will be planned beforehand that way. When the fetus goes back into the light, they will be looked after and will grow up again in heaven.

I am not talking about abortion, Charm. That is something completely different. Abortion is a sin and if needed, I will tell you all about it but not now as it is an extremely complicated subject. Max and I will tell you about abortion, when the time is right, we also have to remember to tell you about child sacrifice, which is one and the same thing. . . also, a sin and 'dark magick,' *(spelt with the letter 'k')*, worshiping satan."

"Babies grow up in heaven?"

"Babies and children grow up very quickly in heaven. They are looked after by family members and other people that excel in childcare. Most will grow to the age of thirty-four in earth years and will stay at that age. That is the same age as Jesus was when he died on this planet. The Elders are thousands of earth years old but still look thirty-four, unless they want to look older or younger."

"When you were in heaven, were there anything that you craved or is there anything in heaven that is lacking?"

"No," they said laughing. "No one is ever hungry, thirsty or in pain. You want for nothing and loneliness and suffering do not exist in heaven."

"Why can't I remember being in heaven?"

"When a person is born, past lives that they have had are not a memory to the majority of people. Usually, you start from scratch, with no memory of them at all. Occasionally, babies and children remember their past life up to a certain age and then the memories fade away as they grow up. It is seldom that people remember into adulthood," V said and continued,

"A few sensitive people do remember snippets of their past lives. It is rare but some people will have spontaneous accent, where out of the blue, at some point in their life, they speak in another accent other than their own. This happens when a traumatic experience occurs in that person's life.

Unintentionally but allowed in heaven for an extra experience. Recollection of one of their past lives comes forward and is remembered, both lifetimes align, their current life folds back and overlaps with their past life for a while. Leaving them with the ability to speak in a different accent, the accent they had in their past life."

"Are there any other abilities people may have that I may not know about?"

"Sometimes a few people will be born with abilities, talents that they had already mastered in an earlier lifetime. In this life, they will remember that talent and remaster it exceptionally quickly at an exceedingly early age. They are called prodigies."

I recall looking at V's orb and saying, "Yes, I have heard about those kids but tell me something very rare, please?"

"Okay. A few people are so focused on remembering their past lives that in the womb, they develop an ability called *'Highly Superior Autobiographical Memory'*. When born, the person can remember absolutely every single thing that has occurred in their life. They never forget anything—nothing at all! This is rare but it happens," she said.

I asked, "What if I don't want to come back here? People are cruel here. Do I have a choice?"

"God sends good people back to be reborn but only if they agree to do so. Every lifetime is a learning experience with some good and some bad people coexisting at the same time."

"Can a child be born bad though? I've heard some stories like that at school?"

"Yes, people born can sometimes be bad at birth. Evil entities might attach themselves to the defenseless fetus, especially if the mother is vulnerable. She may expose herself while pregnant to immoral situations, willingly or forcibly, against her will by other humans. God's gift to us all of having free will plays a huge part in these scenarios and it can get complicated, depending on who is involved.

It depends on the mother's beliefs, her vulnerability or because of other humans forcing her. Through her, the devil can also send out his children into the world. Every soul that is born from God's loving light is accompanied by their own guardian angel, which will constantly fight against evil to save that soul on that person's behalf," V explained.

"Who can help these babies?"

"Their guardian angel can call upon The Council of Elders to send warrior angels, archangels or other souls for help, to battle the evil ones inside of that little person. Guardian angels are in direct contact with those in heaven. Good soul orbs visiting their loved ones, which are spirits souls visiting earth, may also decide to temporarily attach themselves, to help that baby at difficult times of the young person's life's journey. Even though that baby has evil inside them, they also have their guardian angel and other souls that want to help." V replied.

"So, am I right in thinking that spirits can feed on my fear?"

"Yes, there are some unbelievably bad spirits and entities out there that feed on human fear, but these are not God's people. Don't be scared. If you're not scared, they can't hurt you. God's love and light is given to every soul that He chooses, we have this inside of us. Teach them that this love and light will overpower darkness and fear.

It is up to humans to nurture and protect their kids, such as getting them baptized or teaching them prayers of worship to God. At the very least, teach them right from wrong. Do not steal, do not kill, those types of basic things. Temptation is everywhere all of the time, if they follow the right path and do not stray onto the wrong one, they are less likely to face those bad demons and entities that feed on fear."

"So how can you help me in this lifetime?"

"Guardian angels protect people from evil. I'm here to protect you. I will accompany you along every path that you take and I am with you through every decision that you make. For others, guardians are the little voices inside their head that questions their decisions and actions. That little voice is their angel talking to them," said V.

Max added, "A guide, like me, Charm, will tell you the best options to take to accomplish your life's mission. I will put ideas into your head and it is up to you to choose an option. V and I cannot tell you what to do or make you do anything. You have free will if you are not intoxicated and are aware. I will help to guide you back onto a path that can accomplish your own life's goals if you stray too far from it."

V added, "If you are intoxicated, any spirit, entity or demon can step in and take over your body with ease but don't worry, if this ever happens to you, we will step in and keep you safe from harmful spirits. This is your life, Charm, not mine or Max's. We will give you options and feelings to warn you of approaching danger. If you decide not to talk to us, just know that we are the source of that niggly feeling inside of you that something is not right."

she continued, "Few people see their guides or guardians. You are one of the lucky ones. Most people that have Guides dream of them like you dream of Max and me. They recognise their guides because they always look and are dressed the same way. Usually, those dreams are vivid, disturbing or memorable. This is one of the best ways that they have found to guide people. A lot of the times after dreaming premonitions, even though a dream is lived out exactly, most people dismiss it as 'deja-vu' or a 'coincidence' to explain away that dream of upcoming events and not give it a second thought."

"What happens when people die? Where do they go?"

"Let's say we are talking about just you at first,. . . then we can talk about other souls?" Max asked me if that was all right, I nodded and he continued to speak.

"There is a variety of different things that could occur and for countless different reasons. It can get extremely complicated as beings believe differently when living but once in soul form, they will eventually know the truth. V and I will tell you about a few different scenarios, however there are numerous circumstances that could occur.

When you die, your soul leaves your body. Once your soul leaves your body and you see the light; do not be afraid. We suggest that you not hang around on earth, instead go directly towards God in the light. Once your soul steps into God's light, you will feel His unconditional love all around you, then you know that you are safe.

We will be drawn upwards and travel together but at a certain destination, we must leave you. That is when V and I will say goodbye and we will be called back to heaven. We will go most of the way together, then someone else will come for you and will accompany you the rest of the way, we will meet you later, at your life review. If you are an incredibly old soul, you know the way to the light. You may decide to go there yourself and will travel alone without being accompanied."

V explained that different scenarios could occur to a person's soul, she said. "It may be the case that the soul wants to be alone to think about their options when they die. They will stay here on earth as an earthbound spirit until they have made up their mind to go into the light.

"It could be the case that they may not have believed in God when they were living and their soul is scared to go into the light. Their guardian will tell them not to be scared and will encourage them, (in the extremely short time that they have left together) to go into the light, before the guardian must leave the soul behind and journey through the light, that is, if the soul decides to stay on earth.

It could be the case that they may have believed in a different religion, possibly that religion did not practice the belief of the afterlife. The soul may be afraid to go into the light. Before their guardians leave them to return to heaven, they will say goodbye and encourage that soul not to be afraid and to go into the light.

It could be the case that the soul may not realise at first that they are dead. Once over the shock that they, indeed, are dead, they may choose to stay with their loved ones. Unlike people like you, Charm, the majority of the living won't be able to see or hear souls, as they both are in different, *yet parallel dimensions.* The living grieve bitterly for that person who had just died. This is an agonizing scene for any soul to witness. Usually, it is impossible for communication between dimensions, unless a person is sensitive and is on the same frequency, like yourself.

Their guardian will tell the soul not to be scared and will encourage them, in the extremely short time that they have left together, to go with them into the light. Then, normally the guardian must leave the soul behind and journey through the light. That is, if the soul refuses to go.

For whatever reason a soul may decide to stay and just wonder the earth alone, they will be tormented, until they decide to go into the light. If they choose to stay and satan has a reason to take them, this is where and when it will happen. It will be quick. Souls will be tricked into following satan or his dominions. They will not realise that they are in imminent danger. That soul will go with him into the depths of Hell, which is the worst place imaginable, where eternal pain and torture awaits them. It's different with satan. He will take away souls if he has cause to, whether they want to go or not and their free will is lost."

"So, it's up to me if I want to go into God's light and then after my life review, I'll be allowed in heaven. Am I right?"

"All souls still have free will, including you. You can choose to go towards God and step into his loving light or not. Once in His light, you will then remember, know and understand about God and why everything is done in a certain way. Then after, purification, which is normally healing waters. After that, usually, you can enjoy the pleasures of His heavenly realm, which is also called by many names throughout the cosmos and beyond."

"Does God have a name? Who is He and how old is He?"

"God is known by many different names and has many different faces here on earth. This has been since the beginning of everything and will always be. He is the Alpha and the Omega. He is the Eternal Source. God is made of love and without gender! God possesses the entire universe and beyond. He loves all His children within it, whether they love Him or not, whether they believe in Him or not."

I asked V, "What happens when you've gone through the light and are in heaven? What happens next?"

"When you reach heaven, you will have a soul review with one of the angel Elders who is specialised in that job. The book of your life will be opened and there you will see, in movie or play form, what was recorded. It will be every scene in your life. You will see this all around you clearly and is the true documented account of what occurred in your lifetime.

During this time, you will feel the feelings of all the people in the movie. You will hear everyone's thoughts and you will understand how you have affected them in their lives, be it in a positive or in a negative way. Similar to ripples in a pool of water. Then you make judgements on your own actions, which is overseen by the angel who is with you."

"What about the souls that had done bad things on earth? Do they judge themselves too?"

"Scenes involving you, committing unplanned soul group acts, like intentional torture, abortion and murder towards any lifeforms, will definitely be reviewed. In these cases, you will be sent to a place where you must have your soul cleansed before you enter heaven. Your soul will be tainted with sin, and sin is not allowed in heaven. You will sit with multiple Elders from The Council of Elders who will watch your life review. Usually, in the form of a movie with you. Together, you will discuss what happened during your lifetime. They decide what to do next, if you will stay in heaven and if so, which level you will be placed in.

Many factors are taken into consideration. For example, a 13-year-old child was raped, became pregnant and her parents organised an abortion. Another example is a civilian who is innocently trapped in the middle of a war zone. He kills a soldier in self-defense. The soldier was going to kill him, for no reason other than he is ordered to. Regret, repentance and prayers said to the Holy Family because of your bad actions, during your lifetime does help in many situations. Mistakes are made all the time. That's the whole point of life! They must ask themselves, what did they learn from those mistakes or experiences?"

"Do you remember, Charm, last week, what Max told you?"

He said, "If you pray to God for forgiveness for your sins, and are terribly sorry for them, while you are living and breathing on earth. With God's mercy and only if it is *His Will*, you may not be judged for them. You would have already repented and have been forgiven for them. Please remember that God loves you unconditionally and He will not turn away anyone who chooses to go to Him."

"Are there animals in heaven?"

"Jesus promised that He would come back on a white horse, didn't He?" Max said.

"What about a person who takes their own life? What happens to them, V?

"Suicide is a little different. There is a beautiful level in heaven that most suicides must go to first. God is loving and forgiving. He will not abandon anyone who believes in Him and is willing to step into the light. In this level of heaven, there is a school specifically for trauma related to suicide. Everyone here is comforted and here is one of many levels where healing takes place. Elder guides from The Council of Elders will assign a guide to you, who is specialised in suicide-related deaths. Decisions are made with your soul, what to do next after watching your life review with you."

"People who were murdered, what happens to them in heaven?"

V answered, "Victims of murder will be sent to another beautiful level in heaven first, where healing takes place and they can rest. There is a school specifically for murder victims, which will help them to overcome the trauma of dying prematurely. Elder guides from The Council of Elders will assign a guide who is specialised in this field. They will review your life with you.

After you have healed, sweetheart, you will be in the same level of heaven that you were in prior to leaving earth. You will be free to enjoy heaven. If you want to go back to your house, that will be waiting for you. Spend time with the souls from your group and wait for the rest of your soul group to return so that you can discuss that experience with them."

I looked at Max's orb and asked him, "Okay, so say the person's life review went well, what happens next?"

"Usually, if your review goes well, you will meet up with souls that you knew, not just in the life that you just lived but souls from past lives too. They will recognise you and you will recognise people immediately. Huge celebrations take place, which will be organised by your family and friends in preparation for your planned return.

From there, you will be placed in one of the levels in heaven that is most like the stage that your soul has reached, my girl. There, your house will be waiting for you, just the way you left it but now in a different location. You will have time to rest and enjoy that level of heaven. Choices to learn and subjects that you are lacking in to progress to the next level within heaven are offered to you."

"So, what is the goal? Why do you keep coming back, V?"

"Sweetheart, the main goal of every soul is to be an Elder Guide that is specialised in a certain subject that they enjoy the most, to dwell on one of the higher levels nearer to God's glory and love in heaven for all eternity. You choose to learn what pleases God at each level.

The lower the level, the closer to *Gaia,* (earth) and other soul dwelling planets that are similar. Souls on the higher levels can visit the souls on the lower levels but not the other way around. When we speak of levels you seem to think of a staircase or a ladder, this is wrong. Rather, think of going to different countries on a massive globe that you call heaven. Each country is at a different level, in a different place. You travel from place to place after each lifetime."

"Do all in your soul group progress to the next level in heaven together?"

"Hopefully, you are on the same level as your previous soul group and you all progress, learn and grow together as a unit. If not, you are allocated a soul group that best suits you, one that you will be most comfortable with, only for a short while, until you can rejoin your soul group. Elder guides are specialised in allocating soul groups to people on that particular level that you are in. Obviously, you have a choice and the guide will help you through this process."

"What are the schools like in heaven, V?"

"Huge schools for learning with every subject imaginable are taught in every level of heaven. There are subjects from singing, music, carpentry, gardening and drawing.. . . To, the correct way to visit loved ones on earth, and other levels of heaven, or how to appear in dreams, or how to fly etc. There are schools to teach you how to breathe and swim on water planets. How to maneuver on a sandy planet or how to survive on a fiery, scorching hot or freezing, subzero one.

Obviously, depending on your next mission with your soul group. You will learn about what your new body suit will look like for your next mission, how it functions and how your new body will react when faced with certain things. You did not always have a body like the one you have today. You have learned how to live with feathers, wool, scales, fleece, fur, and fins. You have even had a crustacean-like, hard exoskeleton, but now, in this body, you just have clear skin and hair. You are still in the process of practicing how to heal and look after it!

When a soul has learned a particular skill, they can choose another skill to learn. These skills, if you are chosen or volunteer and are allowed to go to a planet, will be carried with you at conception. That's one of the reasons why some young children are gifted on earth, for example, with a beautiful voice or are naturally musical. They could be fantastic at painting or art, outstanding at a particular sport, a whiz at mathematics or history. It could also sometimes be because they recall what they have learned in heaven, or mastered a skill and carried it forward from a past life on a different planet which was in a different dimension."

"What did you and V have to do to become guides and guardians, Max?"

"Souls like mine and V's choose a particular job, my girl. We have to study an exceptionally long time and experience many lifetimes to be able to do the job we have chosen. Other souls prefer to stay in heaven and answer prayer requests. They are called '*Helpers*'. For example, an expert soul in the medical field could be called back by a guardian to help heal someone on earth."

I recall being told about Helpers in a different conversation too. "So, is it just guardians and guides that visit earth, to help living people from heaven then, V?"

"No! There are 'specialised guardian angel Helpers,' who have mastered a single talent. There are so many of them, sweetheart, each individually with a multitude of knowledge in their field, teaching and waiting in heaven to be called upon for a short period of time. They are sent by The Elder Guides who are in communication with all of the guardians everywhere in the universe.

These Elders allocate Helpers to guardians that request assistance. For example, with a person on earth who is very fearful of a situation. In this case, the Helper is matched up to the situation and assists the guardian to calm that person down and together, they protect and comfort them until the crisis is over.

A Helper may be sent for support and to encourage someone to continue a particularly important task, that a person must accomplish in order to complete their goal in life. They may be sent to someone seeking wisdom; inspiration, to overcome sadness, bereavement, for issues with love or to overcome an addiction. This is naming just a few, there are hundreds of thousands of examples, that I can mention that guardian Helpers assist with," she replied.

"Max, will everyone in a soul group go to a planet together? What if some don't want to go and what's the process to be able to go?"

"All souls reside on their levels of heaven, use the comforts and explore the land until their soul group is together again. Usually, souls within their soul group decide that they would like to go to a planet and to learn and grow. Planning and learning is started with the soul group to do that.

Not all souls wait. On occasion, some souls decide that they would like to go back into the same family that is still living their lifespan, on a planet such as earth. They ask to get permission and go through many stages with The Elder Guides, similar to what occurs when a soul group returns to earth. At conception and while developing in their mother's womb, they will have exactly the same personality as before, the same likes and dislikes as before. They may have the skills and features also but different challenges.

If a soul is not ready to leave or does not want to be reincarnated along with their soul group, they do not have to go, they have free will. You will know what you can and cannot do, once you are there, including all of the options available to you."

"How do we know that it is your relative reborn again?"

"When reborn again into that family, traits and likenesses are often recognised by family members of a person that has died. Which, in fact, is the very same soul, but that soul has no memory of that past life! Not everyone has the opportunity to return to live another lifetime. It all depends on their soul's knowledge, accomplishments towards your goal and if God allows them to return. Living a life is a gift to us from God!" Max replied.

"Unwritten" – Natasha Bedingfield (Lyrics)

"Never discourage anyone . . . who continually makes progress. No matter how slow".

Plato

Chapter 12

You Were Born for This

I was curious, so I asked, "So why am I here and what exactly do I have to do, Max?" as I sat on my bed with a pencil and paper, taking notes.

(My notes and from memory)

"Remember, my girl, no evil is permitted within God's kingdom. V and I will protect and guide you through this process. Firstly, you must be extremely careful who you talk to, including the living. You know that there are places called 'mental institutions' on earth, you may hear the place being called a 'mental asylum, lunatic asylum' or a 'psychiatric hospital' amongst other things. Your dad calls the place the *'looney bin'*, it's the same place, just different names. This is where people who hear voices are locked away and given medicines to keep them sedated. The voice of a guide can never be silenced, just softened. If this ever were to happen to you, it's okay. At least you tried. We'll find a way to get you out and will try again later on, in this lifetime or, if unsuccessful, in your next one. So don't worry about that, just be incredibly careful until the time is right.

Once we are all exposed, even then, it will be difficult for you as people will be cruel. They'll say some unkind things. Many will not believe you, even if you have witnesses, who will not stand up and speak the truth to back you up. That's okay too. That's their burden to bear . . . not yours. Do what it says in the Bible. *'Dust them off your feet'* and keep trying . . . Coax souls and people into God's light. Be one of God's instruments, a messenger between heaven and earth.

There will be many hurdles to jump over and you will be judged harshly by humans but the truth will prevail. Nothing can be hidden. One of your missions is to talk to spirits and the living. We're here to help you to do that safely. You must tell all the souls that you meet, the lost souls and earthbound spirits and entities, to *'cry out to God for help'*. He will not abandon them if they are sincere in their plea. They may not want to listen to you but you *must try*!

Advise them to at least consider going into God's light. This is *particularly important*. Tell them and especially the living that demons don't have a soul. However, they can keep demons away if they pray to God and ask Him for protection. God and The Council of Elders will hear their cry for help and will send many angels to protect them from the demons.

Later, when you are older and understand more about the supernatural realm, we will teach you exactly what to say and do when you come across certain demons to disperse them. You are to talk to the living people too. Before you start a reading or have an appointment with the living person, you *must pray to God first for protection* and meditate with them. I will teach you the words for when you are fearful and you already know how to meditate.

You are an instrument of God. Listen to me and speak my words which is in the name of Jesus. I will tell you what messages to say to the living. *Only repeat what I say though.* THIS IS VERY IMPORTANT. Even if you know more about the subject, the living person you are talking to, may not need to know the information you want to tell them at this point in their lives. You will actually be guiding them down another path in their own lives, that they shouldn't be at yet. They have more to learn along their pathway and will miss experiences that were originally planned for them.

You will receive messages from souls that have come from God's light to talk to their living loved ones on earth. Doing this brings *the souls* more happiness and *the living*, some hope and comfort. It will be different for us all when you're communicating with lost and earthbound spirits because I cannot always speak to them, it depends on that individual's skills and what they have learned to do. They will not see or always hear V or me, but we can see and hear them. You have to speak to them yourself. It is what you were sent here to do. It's not because I'm making you speak to them. You have free will.

They will talk to you or play charades and the games that we used to play together. It's up to you, V and me to determine what they want to say. You're good at it now . . . and can piece together their messages. Don't forget to advise them to go into God's light. They will play games if they cannot speak English, or they'll play games if they have not learned how to speak verbally or have not learned how to make you understand through telepathy.

In heaven, a soul could learn how to communicate telepathically with the living. Everyone is telepathic there but to communicate with the living is a completely different subject. When you talk to them, V and I will also guess what they are trying to tell you. I speak many languages and so does V. The spirits, earthbound souls and entities, can become frustrated and even violent and it is V's job to protect you from any bad entities, spirits or souls who could harm you and she's very good at doing her job. Don't mess with V! In this part of my job, I tell you what to say to them and I am surprisingly good at what I do, if I say so myself."

"Yesterday Once More" – Carpenters (Lyrics)

My Aunt Helen and Me

Chapter 13

The Slipper

*A*untie Helen Chance used to visit often and stay for a while at our house. She and her young daughter, Tammy Chance, would sleep on my bedroom floor between the window and the bunk bed on comfortable thick cushions. Aunt Helen had a few spirits that had attached themselves to her. Max, V and I were used to them. They were violent towards her and sometimes would attack her. It was early Saturday morning and we were all sleeping when my Aunt's screams woke the entire household.

She was getting beaten with a slipper by an invisible person. Her daughter Tammy, who was about five years old, Theresa, and I were so scared. I quickly grabbed Hector and leapt off the top bunk. Aunt Helen was now near the desk, nearer to the bedroom door, dodging the blows. The two girls and I quickly huddled together on the bottom bunk. I pushed them in towards the bedroom wall at the back of the alcove in the cupboard space, where the bunkbed nestled. We tried to get as far away from Auntie as possible. I ensured that the two young ones were protected, hiding their faces against my body.

"Is it Reaper, V, that grandpa warned us about?" I asked.

"Sweetheart, hide, hide. It's, it's Reaper, I think, but it can't be. We'll find out. Just keep holding on to them. I can protect all of you with the help of their guardians. Just stay together!" she replied telepathically.

Tony and Mom came sprinting into the room and tried to protect Auntie, who was screaming and trying to cover her head and face with her arms. She had red marks all over her body—legs, face, arms, everywhere. The slipper dropped to the floor and Mom grabbed all of us kids, pushing us out of our bedroom with her as she walked and told us to wait in my brother Tony's tiny bedroom. She left his door open and told him to protect us then ran back to close our bedroom door with Auntie Helen still inside.

Mom ran, grabbed a bottle of Holy Water, which was on the altar in her room and liberally sprinkled it all over our bedroom door in the hallway, around the doorframe of Tony's bedroom and her bedroom doorframe. She went into our room with Auntie and shut the door behind her. I could hear them chanting and praying inside for a while. We can hear our neighbor's Alsatian dogs howling through the walls of our adjacent house. When my Mom and Auntie Helen left the bedroom, Auntie was drenched in Holy Water. She went downstairs, followed by all the children, including myself and my Mom with the bottle still clasped tightly in her hand.

We all sat on the sofas in the living room while Mom went into the kitchen to boil the kettle for some tea for Auntie Helen. She was pretty shaken up by the whole ordeal. Max told me that Reaper had not gone and was still upstairs. Seconds later, Theresa's big red ball bounced step by step down the stairs and hit the glass of the front door below. We all watched it hit the door with force for a second time, then it proceeded to bounce, one step at a time, back up the steps, until out of sight. Mom called our Catholic priest, who rushed over and blessed our house.

***

Auntie Helen was always getting hurt by spirits. I don't know why she didn't go to a priest to be blessed or just for some advice or help. How someone so nice could have something like that around her? To this day, I cannot understand it. V said this entity, Reaper, fed off her fear too and it was unusual as the curse was only for people within our family. Auntie Helen was, in fact, an extremely close family friend and was not a blood relative and had not married into our family.

***

Since our house on Springfield Gardens was blessed, The Spirit Lady in white from next door, The Grey Army Man and The Ghost Girl were seen seldom. My Aunt Jane Frost moved into this house from Coppermead Close, Kilburn, with my three cousins—Gaz, Si and Lea—after us. Mom and Dad had saved up enough money to purchase a home in Kingsbury. Auntie Jane also experienced strange things in the house, at the top of the stairs near the big window she hung a picture.

This picture was always getting turned sideways on the wall. Aunt Jane obviously would turn it back and no matter what she did, the picture would turn by itself, even while she watched it, which freaked her out! Other little things would happen also, such as furniture moving around by itself but after Mom mentioned to Auntie Jane about Aunt Helen, the slipper and ball, Auntie Jane organised for the Catholic priest to come back and re-bless the house before any physical incidents happen.

***

I was reminded by Max and V that hundreds of years ago, a curse was made on the Copper family and a demonic entity that was called Reaper became attached to one of my ancestors. It continued feeding on fear and causing illnesses and havoc within the family, jumping from person to person through generations. Somehow it attached itself to Auntie Helen too and now it's leaping onto people in my own family unit to find a new host. We lost track of the entity and it was residing quietly within one of my family members and feeding.

I was extremely concerned about my little sister Terry. She was so terrified, absolutely petrified, about seeing The Grey Army Man by our bed and now witnessing Auntie Helen being beaten and abused by the entity. Her fear had intensified as we had moved into a new house. Early one morning I had just returned from the bathroom when I could see a dark oval-shaped formation on Terry's back as she lay sleeping on her side.

Reaper was exposed. It had attached itself to my little sister Terry. When it realised I knew it was there, when Terry woke, her personality had changed drastically. She was more fearful than ever, refusing to enter our bedroom alone for weeks after that and slept in Mom and Dad's room. She wouldn't even go to the bathroom herself. Every night I prayed to God and pleaded for Max and V's help to talk to The Council of Elders to get permission that this entity would be removed from my sister and to be banished from our family.

Eventually, after months of trying, I was informed by Max that the Elders would send an angel to Terry, but only if I promised that I would take Reaper upon myself. If I agreed, I was told that my life's plan would be altered but not drastically. The Elders told Max that Reaper's curse was put onto a man within our family. It cannot be removed because of the law of free will. It is up to our family to find out his real name and rid ourselves off this entity through prayer or exorcism from certain Catholic priests who are trained for this job. Until then Reaper is bound to our family.

They told Max that the agreement would be, if I approved to take on the entity, Terry will receive an extra angel called Michael until he is not needed to be with her anymore. I will just have him and V to protect me. Together, we planned on how we would go about banishing Reaper from the family altogether. Max had some ideas and we were all set to take on the challenge.

"Theresa will, however, still have strong feelings and will be able to sense souls near her but won't see or hear them. This is a family inheritance that cannot be broken. All parties involved have approved the change, including little Theresa in a dream state. What do you want to do, my girl?" Max asked me.

V spoke, "Charm, this is rare. The Elders will only allow Michael in exceptional circumstances, sweetheart. He is an *Archangel*, a warrior. Please make your decision carefully. We'll honour your choice."

"Are you okay with this? Can you both handle Reaper when he is on me?" I asked.

"Neither Max nor I have been trained for this but we do have the Elders who can send more help if we need it."

"So that's a yes then. I will be helping her, right? Terry will be safe?" I asked.

"It won't be easy for you, Max and I but yes, Theresa's life will be a normal one. She will live with just the challenges she has chosen and those given to her originally by the Elders. Reaper will not go near her if Michael is here," V replied.

We discussed the new challenges we would have, combatting the entity. I insisted we do this and told Max and V I couldn't see my sister suffer like that and be so fearful. Plans were rolling in heaven and with Max, V and me. We had another family party to attend the next day and while we were there, I noticed Reaper leaving my sister and jumping on my Auntie Edna, my cousin Jen's Mom, who was my godmother. It turned out Terry wasn't the entity's target after all and that Auntie Edna was his next victim.

"Good luck to it. Auntie Edna is a tough cookie to chew!" I said to Max and V.

***

We had a lucky escape and I didn't have to be reminded that this entity will keep feeding on my family members and causing trouble, unless stopped but how? After that day, I stayed away from my sister as much as I could and when I was in our bedroom with her, I kept the radio off. She was extremely tired and took a few daytime naps while I secretly watched over her from my side of the room. Reaper had not come near Terry during our following family parties and I had lost track of who the entity was feeding on after a while. All the plans for me to take on the Reaper entity were put on hold until it reappeared.

"Sister" – Mickey Guyton (Lyrics)

Nee, Mari and Me

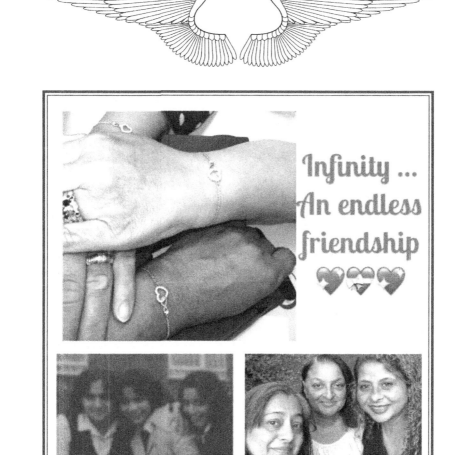

From left to right, Mari, me and Nee when we were younger and carefree. From left to right in the lower photo, Mari, Nee and me, not so young but still carefree! This photo was taken in 2022, when we met up, then Mari surprised us with gifts, an 'Infinity Bracelet' each. These are our wrists wearing our bracelets in the photo. This friendship has survived the test of time. My bracelet, I will treasure for the rest of my life.

"Yesterday is history,
tomorrow is a mystery,
today is a gift of God,
which is why we call it the present."

Bil Keane

Chapter 14

High School

Mom and Dad bought a house on Berkeley Road in Kingsbury when I was in my early teens. They'd started to pay a mortgage and worked harder than ever to make this house a home. Racism at that time in my life was one of the huge obstacles I faced living in that area of London. Max advised me a lot then. At Kingsbury High School, I not only faced verbal abuse but also physical from children at my school. The teachers there, even though kind and vigilant, didn't have a clue that bullies wreaked havoc in the playground and within the hallways. They didn't know how bad it was there for people of colour, pushing, shoving, name-calling and stealing dinner money.

Our English teacher, Ms. Parker, was in tears most days. She would be bullied because she was overweight and because of the way she dressed. I learned martial arts and how to defend myself, which was often, especially after school, walking home. I had two best friends since "Olly Golly" school, as we used to call it. Neena,

Marisha and I were all getting bullied because of our brown skin colour. Kids used to say to us remarks like, "Hey, packies, why don't you go back to your own fucking country?"

I had heard those words or words similar to them since elementary school and became accustomed to them. It was on the occasions when the kids became violent and asked us for fights that concerned me the most. We defended one another and stuck together constantly. I felt at times that we were like young zebras surrounded by a pack of hungry lions, always taunting us, circling around us and threatening to pounce. They would often say, "Wanna fight? Cum-on, packies, yes, you fuckers are all alike, fucking come here and take our jobs. You're all a bunch of fuckers."

Everything changed when Neena and I signed up for judo. After a few years of that, it was after Nee and I went to the judo championship competition for Brent that the physical bullying stopped for all of us. I came in third and won a bronze medal and a little silver cup. The verbal abuse towards us was still continuing from a distance but by then, we were all so used to being called "packie." The word was ignored and we didn't retaliate.

"Sticks and stones could break your bones but words can never harm you," my parents used to tell me.

***

These words ran through my mind often and not just for situations with the living. Confidence in myself started building. I thought I could take care of myself and did not need Max's or V's advice much. I was still in plenty of pain on my face periodically and it continued to swell up to the size of my fist, just under my ears and the swelling would recede a few days later. I was still seeing doctors and was referred to a few E.N.T. specialists. I started to get new pains in my legs, which didn't help diagnose what was wrong with me.

"That's What Friends Are For" – Dionne Warwick (Lyrics)

Chapter 15

Ouija Board

The start of junior high at Kingsbury High was pretty uneventful. I hadn't spoken to Max and V much and their voices were faint in my head. I was avoiding having conversations with my guide and guardian because the thought of seeing and helping creepy ghosts like the ones in the dog alleyway really freaked me out. Hearing them didn't bother me that much and I still saw the orbs, spirits and entities but I was used to them. I was okay as long as I didn't look at them. That way, they thought I was like everyone else and couldn't see them, so they left me alone.

I was working on how to control my thoughts at night but was unsuccessful as they still bothered me in my dreams and some woke me from my sleep. A few of the kids in my year regularly played around with a Ouija board at lunchtimes. It was played in a small room used to store brooms and cleaning supplies. One of the boys was great at unlocking the door's little padlock with a paper clip or a bobby pin. It was easy access for them and the door locked from the inside, which was a bonus for them. I was invited a few times to join in but Max was insistent.

"Don't mess around with it. Really bad things could happen. You do know it's a direct line to the spirit world, don't you?"

Curiosity got the better of me and defiantly, I joined in once with them. The pine-coloured wooden board was slipped out from behind a stack of shelves. It was placed on the floor in the middle of the room and a clear water glass was placed on it upside down. It took seconds to set up the game.

"How did the board get in here? The board is big," I asked a boy as he was entering the room.

"The cleaner's (janitor's) son snuck it in one night, excuse me," he said as he moved in front of me to the far side of the room and knelt on the floor then sat on his feet, facing the board.

One after the other, people came in, nine of us in total. There was not enough room for us all to be on the floor. Six where kneeling around the printed board, which was beautiful, smooth and shiny, complete with numbers, words and letters on it. The glass was scooted to the center of the board and four people put a finger on the top of the glass.

"Hey, Charm, do you want to try?" Paul asked.

"Sure, but you have to tell me what I have to do. I've never done this before," I replied, changing places with Paul quickly.

He stood behind me nearest to the door and was explaining briefly how the game worked.

"Just put your finger on the glass's bottom gently and keep it there. Follow the glass."

The glass started to spin with the three kids and me touching it.

I played for a while and watched everyone take turns to put a finger on the glass. When it was my turn to remove my finger, the glass stopped spinning immediately, causing everyone's fingers to slip off it. They tried again and once it started to spin, a question was asked by one of the girls next to me.

"Are you a good spirit or a bad spirit?"

The glass kept spinning faster and faster in the center of the board and didn't point to any words or letters. It was my turn again to touch the glass. After a few minutes, it was awkward for me to keep my hand on the glass as it spun so fast. My arm was getting tired. I decided to swap places with Paul again. I was heading to take my place back near the door, when I noticed some commotion behind me and realised the glass had stopped abruptly.

They started playing again while I watched the glass spin slowly in the middle of the board.

"What is your name?" a boy asked while standing next to me.

The glass slipped towards Paul and everyone opposite had to stretch and get up onto their knees to keep their finger on the glass, then it went back into the middle of the board. The glass slipped again towards Paul. The same thing happened. Everyone had to stretch to stay on the glass. It looked like a wave with bodies rising and falling and back again. This occurred about five or six times and everyone was laughing, including me.

"What is your name?" a boy asked with his finger placed gently on the glass.

It started spinning furiously in the middle of the board and they swapped people on the glass. It spun faster and faster then stopped on the letter G.

"G," everyone said together.

"Okay, Charm, funs over. I suggest you leave now. I'm not getting a good feeling about this. Max is concerned too," V said.

I ignored them and kept watching.

"Unlock and open the door, watch from the hallway. It's not safe in here," V said.

The glass moved to the letter E and I was curious to what the message was.

"E," everyone said together, including me.

What names start with GE? I was confused and couldn't think of many.

"George, maybe?" I said, hoping the glass would go to the word *Yes* on the board.

The glass spun a little bit and it landed over the letter T.

"T!" everyone shouted together.

"GET OUT, Charm, it's a warning," Max said.

I listened to Max and unlocked the door, just in case. Then the glass quickly spelled the letters O, U, T.

"O-U-T," everyone said together.

"Get out," Paul said, laughing.

"Who the fuck is doing it?" he asked as the glass was spelling GET OUT over and over at such a speed that one by one, fingers were removed from and replaced back on the glass. It was impossible to touch and follow it around as it zipped over the board at a tremendous speed.

Everyone was laughing as they were still trying to catch the glass with their pointers. I had my hand on the doorknob and opened the door slowly and quietly.

"NO!" everyone shouted together.

I quickly closed it shut. Their unexpected voices echoed, which made me jump a little.

"NO, NO, NO, NO," everyone kept repeating as I turned to watch the glass, now pointing to the word *No* on the board, moving away and pointing to the word *No* again.

"We suggest you leave NOW! This place is not safe for you," V said.

I reopened the door and was walking out when Paul stood up and spoke in disbelief to the crowd on the floor,

"This is a load of shit, someone's pushing that glass!"

He turned to me and was about to leave after me when the glass flew off the floor like a bullet and cut the tip of his left ear off, then the missile headed for me. I was already out of the room by then. The glass smashed and lay shattered on the floor outside in the hallway behind me.

As I turned to see Paul holding his ear in shock, pushed by him were the other kids trying to get out of the room. I could hear rumbling as the board was trembling on the floor. The kids just wanted to get out of there as quickly as they could, stepping on the broken glass; with imbedded shards on their souls, they tracked glass pieces up the hallway with them as they scattered in different directions.

***

The school nurse saw Paul. He went home for the rest of the day. The next morning there was a different type of lock on that utility door.

"So, what happened to the board?"

I asked Paul and the people who were in that room with me. No one knew what had happened to it. It was possibly tucked back behind the stack of shelves.

I was in tons of pain around this time, which affected my legs and arms but this didn't stop me from playing sports, such as badminton, with a male classmate at school; this guy, I actually had a crush on. Even though he hung around with Nee, Mari and me a lot, I didn't think he liked me any more than a good friend but I liked him more than that.

"Jump the Line" – Harry Belafonte (Lyrics)

Earlier Year's Holiday Pics

Tony, seven years old; Terry, two years old, is in her stroller at the front of the photo; and me, six years old. Tony and I are standing on either side of the Butlin's Holiday Camp Giant in Bognor Regis.

I came second place at a beauty contest when I was ten years old, no. 14 at Butlin's

12 years old, I came first place in the beauty contests, three years in a row at Butlin's

1ˢᵗ prize in the Donkey Derby Race Photo
13 years old, I came first place racing my donkey at the donkey derby contest in Butlin's

My brother Tony, 15 years old and me, 14 years old, in Spain

My Photo

*My photo was taken by a close
family friend, 24 October 1982.*

Chapter 16

Kilburn College

*B*y the tender age of fifteen, I learned how to block out all the spirits' voices to an incredibly quiet whisper, including my guide and guardian, even though they would persist in talking to me in my dreams. When we'd meet up, I'd see and hear them as clear as day. There, most of the time at my request, they taught me how to avoid telepathic conversation, communication and a certain way to avoid eye contact with the dead and I became exceptionally good at them all, but I still saw soul orbs.

***

When I went to view the college, it was definitely haunted, but I liked it and decided I would spend two years there studying. It became easier for me to ignore the spirits and to get on with my studies. I decided to do an "audio secretarial and shorthand typing course" the first year. Then on the second year, I would study "business education." However, when I did start college, the orbs were distracting and they were my biggest downfall but as time elapsed, all the voices became faint, which, at that time, I thought was a blessing.

***

Max and V, in orb form, would always hover discretely near me at all times, which I very much appreciated. I hardly noticed they were there until they'd whisper advice to me upon my request. This was usually when I was scared or indecisive when making an important life's decision. Neena and Marisha chose other paths and we struggled to stay in contact and hardly spoke to one another, which was very painful to me as I missed them so much. I missed Nee's jokes and Mari's contagious giggle.

***

Spirits and orbs flew through the corridors of the college in vast amounts, darting around the students who studied there. A few scary earthbound spirits hung around the students who were on drugs or who drank alcohol heavily, hoping they could jump into their bodies as soon as they were high or paralytic drunk. They would hang around people, hanging on to them like dark matter when the person is hungover the next day, reluctant to leave their host.

So many times, people would say to me, "I can't remember that I did that!" or "She's so different when she drinks," or "He only beats me when he's drunk."

Yes, it's probably because it's not them but someone dead, a lost soul, earthbound spirit or a demonic entity similar to Reaper, using them to experience life and to live again, such as to have sex or cause havoc and illnesses. It is easy for spirits and entities because when intoxicated, there is no resistance from that person. A lot of the orbs, entities and spirits at college are between fifteen and twenty years old. They are not usually there to learn subjects taught but mostly there to hang around students, watching them interact with one another and the majority of them cause no problems at all.

A few are stuck a in loop, always doing the same thing over and over and over again. I don't know why this happens or if they would ever be able to move into the light. They do not know that time has elapsed. They wear the same old-fashioned clothes, all from different eras. In the past, the lower half of the building may have been some type of hospital or medical place; a lady dressed in a white nurse's uniform walks through walls there.

In another part of the building, a fireman also ran through, so there might have been a fire there at some point in the past. Travelling there every weekday by buses in the mornings and doing the same journey home, the route of one of the red double-decker buses went under a large brick bridge, which was Kilburn train station on Kilburn High Road. It was a few bus stops away from where I would get off and walk to the college. There were trains running across the top of the bridge on a regular basis, every five minutes or so. Going under that bridge arch made me really nervous. I think someone may have died there or maybe it was me who died in my past life, involving a bridge and train. I don't know but I felt like it was an accidental death. Nevertheless, I was fearful approaching the bridge and was relieved once the bus passed under it.

***

It was around this time when my E.N.T. specialist doctors decided there was nothing wrong with me and referred me to a dentist, who decided to replace some of my silver mercury fillings just in case those were causing the pain and while I was under general anesthetic, they dug in and took out all my wisdom teeth. When I recovered from that, I was still in pain and the random and intermittent swellings on either side of my face didn't subside. The pain in my legs started transferring to my fingers and elbows and worked its way haphazardly around my body. On one day, I would have pain in my left leg, then the next morning the pain in my leg would subside and I would have pain in my right elbow.

***

At home, I practiced the latest dance moves in my bedroom to keep fit. I would sketch and draw. Still, my favorite pastime was listening to my music. Writing down lyrics on those little white cards from the sunroom of our old house, while I listened to the radio or my music tapes. On weekends, I'd often visit Jen, my cousin at her house. A few times I would go on blind double dates with Jen and her boyfriend and his male friend. We would go out together on a date as it was safer in pairs being teenage girls.

I'd catch the 183 red double-decker bus from Kingsbury High Road and travel to West Harrow, dump my overnight bag at her house and we'd sometimes go places, see her friends, go to discos or go on one of these blind double dates. This is where I met Raymond (Ray). We dated for about a week. He'd meet me at Kingsbury Station. We'd go to restaurants or walk around the shops in Kingsbury. He was in his late twenties and I was only sixteen and had just started college. After getting to know him a little, he really wasn't my type and I broke up with him.

"In the Summertime" – Shaggy (Lyrics)

Chapter 17

Boys

*M*om and Dad couldn't afford expensive holidays and would take our family to *Butlin's* every year. I think that the location, operations and structure of the movie *Dirty Dancing* was based on this holiday camp. Nearing the end of our long road trip there, we would look out for the huge giant man figure, which overlooked a fun fair. This huge being stood prominently at the camp's gates. There were hundreds of chalets (flats) for the holidaymakers to reside in. The main square had many different shops, an ice cream parlour, where we would get our family's favorites. I loved to watch people swimming underwater from a window as I ate my knickerbocker glory sundae.

There was a souvenir shop where Mom would buy her shell ornaments and sticks of candied rock as holiday gifts for my cousins back home. A photography shop where you would buy photos from the professional photographer who would roam around the grounds capturing the memories of the campers there. He would be at every important event I entered into, the donkey derby race in a large field, the talent and beauty contests in a large hall, dance competitions, all of them.

That swimming pool, where I would watch people swim while eating my knickerbocker glory sundae, is where we took swimming and diving lessons. I recall my Dad saving me from drowning while teaching me how to swim there. There was a communal launderette my Mom tried to avoid and a TV room my Dad longed to visit often to rest. All the helpers at Butlin's that worked there were called "Red Coats," and that's what they wore too.

Some would assist the children in the Beaver Club while the adults did what adults do during the day. There were multiple competitions—fancy dress, beauty, talent, dance and so many more—in the outdoor areas too. Entertainers and community activities were scattered throughout the grounds. We were hardly ever bored. We went back to Butlin's every year for many fantastic vacations.

Each chalet (flat/apartment) had their own allocated table in the dining hall. I was sixteen and it was my first break off from college. This is where we met Mick, who was 25 years old. He waited at our table. Mick was having a challenging time as he couldn't find work as a mechanic in that area and took the job at Butlin's until he found a place to work. Mom made a few phone calls to her sister Jane as she knew her husband was looking for a mechanic to work with him in his shop in Cricklewood. Dad invited Mick to come and live with us as a lodger as they needed some extra cash for bills. We all got on really well with Mick while vacationing for two weeks at *Butlin's in Bognor Regis, UK.*

***

Back at home in Springfield Gardens, Mick moved in and we all lived together. The arguments started when Mick wanted to date me. He persisted relentlessly. Eventually, I agreed. I went back to college after a short break. I met Raj for the first time. He was sixteen too and was in my class. We got on really well together and he asked me to go out with him. I agreed immediately and went home to tell Mick I wanted to break up with him.

Mick was furious when I told him. He slapped and started beating me on my head and arms then proceeded to throw things across my bedroom. I became afraid of him and after that, I tried avoiding him every chance I could. I never told my parents what had occurred that day. Raj was Hindu and was not allowed to have a girlfriend. His elder sister was also at college. She would keep an eye on him to ensure he wasn't doing anything to upset their parents. Raj and I had to keep our relationship as quiet as possible but meanwhile, I was falling deeper in love with him with every day that went by.

One day, as we were in the college hallway, we saw his sister approaching and we quickly ducked into the men's bathroom. Realising what we'd done, the only option was to go into one of the bathroom stalls there. I was frightened that I'd get caught, so he hugged and kissed me to comfort me. Boys were in and out constantly and we were in there for some time. What a place to lose your virginity!

***

My Dad's niece, Bindu, from India came to stay for a few months. She slept on a single mattress on the floor of our bedroom, near the bunk bed next to Theresa. She was nice and we spoke often about her life in India. She told me she wanted to live in England and that my Mom and Dad were willing to sponsor her to enable her to stay. Mick hardly spoke to me; he would spend most of his time in his room within the sunroom downstairs. I was happy about that and was overjoyed when I came to find out from my parents that he had given notice to move out.

Shortly after Mick moved out, Bindu did too. We had a lot more room in the house and the atmosphere was pleasant. A month had passed, though and I was concerned that I hadn't had my period. It usually came like clockwork. I was late by about two or three weeks. I plucked up the courage and spoke to my Mom about it. She was extremely disappointed in me and wanted to tell my Dad. I begged her not to.

The next morning Mom took me to the doctor who told us that, indeed, I was pregnant. He suggested I abort the baby. Mom looked into my options and we spoke for the following days about it. I felt sick to my stomach and I was so scared. I couldn't breathe. I couldn't think or make any important decisions and I turned to V and Max to help me make up my mind. Should I keep the baby, give the baby up for adoption or kill my child?

"Charm let's pray to God together for Him to give me the right words to tell you," V said.

V, Max and I prayed. They hovered as orbs, one on each of my shoulders, as I knelt and prayed in my Mom's room at the altar.

"It will all be okay, don't worry, Charm. This is all part of God's plan for you. You have an exceedingly difficult road to walk down, sweet girl, just be brave and keep your baby, don't kill," V said.

"We're with you on your journey, all the way until the end, don't be sad," Max said.

***

The next day Mom had planned for me to go to talk to someone about abortion, which was one of my options and we were in the clinic's bathroom before the appointment. I was nervous and started biting my nails. She handed me a fag and said softly while hugging me in her arms,

"Here, baby, I know you smoke, I've known for years. Moms have to pick our battles and this is not the right time to lecture you on smoking again, honey. This is the first and last time I'll hand you one. You need this just as much as I do right now, babe. Remember, whatever you decide, I'm on your side. I've decided that this will be our secret, unless you decide to keep your baby, okay? Until then, I won't tell your father. I will walk this road with you, Charm. You are not alone. Please tell me, who's the father?"

I didn't get a chance to thank her for being with me, for keeping my secret or who the father was as we could hear my name being called by the nurse from outside in the waiting room. We took a huge drag in of our fags, stubbed them out and ran them under the water before chucking them in the bin. After the appointment, we knew this was not going to be an option for my child. Shortly after, back in Kingsbury, we caught our transportation; me, a bus to college and Mom, a Jubilee line by underground train from Kingsbury Station to her work at the *Hong Kong Government Office* in Green Park.

***

The next day Mom left early for work as she had taken a little time off the day prior and I was getting ready for college, braiding my hair upstairs, alone in the house, when V flew in front of my reflection in the mirror and said faintly, "Lock the front door."

"I did already," I replied.

Then I heard the front door close and footsteps coming up the stairs.

"Tony, Terry!" I called out, thinking that either my brother or sister had forgotten something and returned home to pick it up.

"No, it's me." I knew Mick's voice.

He stood at my bedroom door. In seconds, I picked up my college bag and put it on my shoulder. My eyes squinted and my lips straightened tight as I stood facing him. With my hands on my hips.

I said, "I'm sure I locked the door. You should ring the bell or knock or something before coming into this house. You don't live here anymore. You can't just walk in! Why are you here?"

"Your Dad should have changed the locks. I came to talk to you," he said.

"What the hell! Give me back the key. You have no right to be here. Leave the key and go!"

"You'll have the key back if you talk to me. I need to tell you something," he said.

"Call me on the phone, write me a letter, there's other ways to talk to a person. Give me the key!" I said as I pushed past him.

Feeling vulnerable now, I knew I had to leave my bedroom and go downstairs, nearer to the front door. He caught me by my shoulder and pulled me back slightly, causing my bag to fall onto the last step. He was directly behind me as I walked towards the door and reached to open it for him as a huge hint to go.

"Stop, wait, we need to talk," he said, pulling me back up against the coats hanging high on a coatrack at the bottom of the stairs nearest to the front door. While pinned up against the fringes of the coats, his hands on my shoulders and facing me.

He blurted out quickly, "I love you. Please, can we work this out? I can't live without you. I love your family."

With eyebrows raised and now getting upset, with tears in my eyes, I wiggled and shrugged his hands off my shoulders. He let go of me.

I said, crying out, "Yeah, so you love me, right? Is this the way you treat everyone you love, Mick, to slap and beat them? Just get out of my house!"

He held his palms up to me and lowered his head, saying, "Just one chance, one. I'm sorry I put my hands on you just now. I'm sorry that I hit you. Fuck, I'm so sorry about that. Please, I'll never touch you like that again."

His eyes welled up with tears and he reached for my hand to hold it. Quickly, I pulled my hand towards my chest and said to him, "It will never work between you and me. I'm in love with someone else and I'm having his baby. I just found out that I'm pregnant. He doesn't know yet."

I was now in a rolling cry, sobbing and blubbering, wiping the tears off my face with my jumper sleeve. He took a step back and shook his head.

"No . . . no," he said, stepping back again. He reached up and touched the door with the palm of his left hand and pointing to me with his right, he said, "I fell in love with you from the moment I saw you. Moved here to be with you. Now you're pregnant? Fuck, girl!"

He left me crying near the coats and he bolted upstairs into the bathroom, saying, "Fucking bitch! You're a fucking bitch! You couldn't wait for me. You promised that if we wait until you're eighteen, we would . . ."

I heard V's voice faintly saying, "Leave now. You're right near the door, sweetheart. Go now before he comes back. Grab your bag. Go catch your bus!"

I reached for my coat and picked up my college bag from the bottom step. When opening the door, I could hear the rumbling of Mick flying down the stairs and in a second, he pushed the door close from behind me.

Stunned, I stood looking at the glass door. He flipped me around; my bag fell again as he was punching me repeatedly in the stomach. His hands were bleeding on my jumper. I tried pushing him away. I tried holding his hands and wrists, which were covered in streaks of blood. I looked up to see his eyes were black and in between his chipped teeth, he had a razor blade.

"Please . . . please not my stomach. The baby, the baby!"

Blow after blow I took with his clenched fists, I tried crouching down low to protect my belly, with my back up against the glass door, my hands over my head to shield my face from him. After hitting me on the head a few times and out of breath, he stopped.

"He's done, I think," Max said.

"He's done, we think, sweetheart. Are you okay? Charm, you can look now. We need to see your face. You need to see what he's doing," V said sympathetically.

I relaxed a little, opened my clasped eyes, dropped my exhausted arms and slowly lifted my head. I thought I saw stars at first but they transformed into hundreds of orbs. Some were floating all around me and some were motionless, forming a wall like barrier between Mick and me.

I looked down at my belly then at my hands, hearing Max softly saying, "The blood is not yours."

Now hearing grunting and huffing that muffled Max's voice, I could see Mick slashing his wrist violently with the razor blade, swapping it from hand to hand and really working on ripping through his skin while gasping and groaning as he sliced.

V whispered in my right ear, "Get up, leave. Leave now. You are in danger. Quickly, now."

I sprung to my feet, grabbed my bag and left running out of the house, looking over my shoulder every now and then, hoping he wouldn't follow me. I ran to the phone box to call my Mom and tell her what had happened, then I ran for the bus, which I could see approaching from a distance. Once on the bus, I knew I had to get to college. There, they have security guards and I'd be safer. The pain in my belly wasn't subsiding. It was getting worse. My arms and head weren't that bad. They ached a little.

I walked slowly from the bus stop to the college. I was in pain. When I got to the college, even though I was late, I stopped and told the security guards what had happened. They called the principal and I waited in the office for a while. I was concerned I was tardy but the principal reassured me that everything would be okay. The phone in her office rang and it was my Mom, calling her to tell her to watch out for me. They chatted for a while and once she hung up the phone, she told me my Mom was on her way and it will take her about an hour to arrive.

She also called Raj out of class for me. When he arrived, the principal was kind enough to let us talk in a vacant classroom alone together. I told him I was pregnant with his child and about the beating I had just received from Mick. I needed to use the bathroom and he accompanied me there and waited outside for me. In there, my panties were covered in blood. I was shocked and screamed out hysterically to him. He came bursting in while I was still sitting on the toilet.

I was embarrassed but he helped me stand up and said he would be with me when we went to see the nurse. As I stood, blood streamed down my white pants and the pain, the awful pain.

"Babe, I'm going to get the nurse. Wait here. I love you. It will be okay. I won't be long," Raj said.

Two girls came into the bathroom. When they saw me, one stayed with me and the other waited outside the entrance to the bathroom, to stop other girls from entering. I could hear people running. Raj and the nurse came in with a wheelchair. A security guard was with them. He had a walkie-talkie and was talking to another security guard, saying, "We'll be out the front in about five minutes. Let us know when the ambulance arrives."

They helped me onto the wheelchair and ran with me down the hallways to the security guard station, where I had to walk a little onto another wheelchair waiting for me on the other side of the turnstiles. As we approached the college doors, ambulance men were bringing in a stretcher. In enormous pain, I managed to get up onto it and into the vehicle. Sirens wailing, and orbs rushing all around me, some were going in and out of my belly while Raj held my hand in the ambulance.

"Our baby will be okay. Don't worry, I'll marry you. I'll marry you right away, okay? We can raise this child together, don't worry," he said to me.

I was in extreme pain, unimaginable pain, which came in waves. I couldn't think, I couldn't speak. I just wanted it to stop! The ambulance men rushed me straight through triage into a little room where a doctor was waiting for me. Two nurses were there also. One took my vitals and the other helped me take off my jumper. An I.V. was inserted into my arm as the doctor examined my stomach with his hands, then he used a machine. He asked for my shoes, socks and pants to be removed. I was wearing nothing, except a white sheet, as he gave me an internal exam. I screamed in pain as my Mom came in and saw Raj holding my hand during the procedure. The doctor removed his hand.

"Son, you need to leave and wait outside," the doctor told Raj.

"But, doc, she's having my baby. I'm going to marry her," Raj said.

"Her mother's here. You need to leave, son. I'm sorry."

"But, doc, cum on, this is so wrong," Raj objected.

"It's policy, son. One person only and because you are not related to this patient, this lady takes priority."

Raj waited somewhere in the hospital while my Mom sat with me through the internal exam. The doctor leaned over me and said to me, "I'm sorry, dear but we must take the fetus. There is no hope here, no other option, I'm afraid. We have to do it right now."

"No, please," I begged. "Please don't take my baby from me, just stop the bleeding," I pleaded.

"My dear, I'm sorry to tell you there is no hope. We don't think that your baby is alive anymore. If I don't take the fetus, you will most surely bleed out. This must be done."

He looked at my Mom, who was crying just as much as I was, as they raised my opened legs and placed them up high with straps on my feet to hold them in position. We were sobbing and Mom cradled my face with her body, we wept bitterly together as the forceps and instruments entered my body.

"It's all my fault, Mom, I killed my baby."

"No, no, sweetheart, you didn't do anything wrong, Charm."

"Mom, please tell them to stop. I want to keep my baby."

"Is there anything that you can do to save my grandchild, please? We don't care how much it costs. Save her baby."

The doctor looked down at me and said with the softest of voice, "Your baby has already been taken, my dear. You need to keep still. You are bleeding a lot."

"Charm, we can help you. Will you come with us?" V said softly in my ear.

"Yes," I replied.

I sat with Max and V in our place. It was white everywhere, including the bench on which we were sitting. I held my child in my hand, pink, in a fetal position, at ten weeks. He was recognisable as a human baby boy and I knew he was still alive as he was moving while lying silently on his side on my palm. He was warm to the touch and his features were not formed completely yet.

We all sat there crying, looking at him. I saw three women approaching us, all wearing floor-length deep V-neck, creamy golden, sleeveless dresses. I have never seen that colour before. All were barefoot and wore their hair in a large, neat bun on top of their heads. They looked like triplets, very pretty but it was easy to tell them apart because of their slight feature differences.

They stopped and smiled at me, then the middle one took a few steps closer and put her hands together. Cupping them one under the other, she reached out to me.

"Goodbye, my son, wait for me. I'm so sorry that I couldn't protect you."

"My Heart Will Go On" - Celine Dion (Lyrics)

*Permanence, perseverance and persistence
in spite of all obstacles,
discouragements, and impossibilities: It is this, that in
all things distinguishes the strong soul from the weak."*

Thomas Carlyle

Chapter 18

All about V

Max would often show me visions of V. She was fair skinned with a beautiful unblemished complexion. Always surrounded by a dazzling glow, her aura was hazy and white. She had long wavy blond hair. I could never tell what colour her eyes were. V told me they were blue.

Her dress looked like a wedding dress. It was long and white. It swayed like silk with graceful light movements as if a gentle breeze were always upon her. Her dress had a low rounded neckline starting just above her cleavage, curving nicely around, barely touching the tips of her shoulders, around to her back covering her shoulder blades. The dress hugged her figure around her breasts to her waist.

Her sleeves were like shimmering, delicate semi-transparent lace that flowed easily over her arms to her wrists. There, it was banded and continued on as fingerless gloves made from the same material wrapped over her palms and around half of her thumbs. Folds of material were used to make the sleeves and somehow they were attached to her dress under her arms on both sides because when she lifted her arms above her head, the underside of her sleeves would stay put at her hips, and the folds of material would fan out, resembling semi-transparent angel wings.

V had a slender, hour-glass figure and wore a thick white ribbon swooping tightly around her waist, which was tied in a neat large bow on her back. The bow's tail cascaded down her dress, stopping just before the hem. Below the wide ribbon around her waistline descended a lightly pleated silk skirt that stopped just below her ankles. She wore no shoes on her feet but they were always clean.

"I Dreamed a Dream" – Susan Boyle (Lyrics)

Venus's (V's) Orb

V, my guardian angel, is happy to meet you! In this photo, she is in orb form. She is the brightest orb on the chair. We were all celebrating together on a special occasion at a party within our house.

I have enlarged her photo so you can see her more clearly.

" O divine Master, grant that I may not so much
seek to be consoled as to console.
To be understood as to understand.
To be loved as to love.
For it is in giving that we receive.
It is in pardoning that we are pardoned,
and it is in dying that we are born to eternal life."

Francis Of Assisi

Chapter 19

Venus

*I*n later years, around the time when I started elementary school, I spoke to my parents and told them that I wanted to change my name. It was due to the fact that the kids in the playground teased me about mine. They used to make me cry. V explained that in one of her previous lives, when she was born, her name was Venus and she hated it.

Kids her age used to tease her too about her name. They would say she was named after one of many goddesses because of her beauty. This is not the same Venus we know of today. Her hair was black, she had very dark brown, nearly black eyes and her skin was the colour of dried sand, which was much lighter than all her other family members.

***

When she was small, the kids made her cry. They fell to their knees, bowing and pretending to worship her. They had done this every time they saw her and every chance they had. She was beaten by her father because of this as he thought it was a game she participated in willingly. Eventually, she told her mother's youngest sister what was happening, but V died shortly after because of the injuries received from the last beating her father gave her due to this cruel game.

After many conversations with my guardian, wanting to know more about this lifetime, I had found out she was an Israelite in Egypt around the time of Pharoah Ahmose. His name translates to "the moon is born," and V said it was the brother prince of Moses. Pharoah Ahmose had a son called Prince Sapair, who died by the hand of God at around eleven or twelve years old in 1500 BCE. Then around the 18th dynasty, V lived in a city called Hyksos, the capital of Avaris, which was told is north of Cairo. There, a river from the Nile branched off and travelled through her lush city.

She lived when the sky rained down fire and ice and then lost all its light. V told me, when she died, she found out God caused a volcano to erupt in a place called Santorini, which caused a chain of events, plagues and darkness. She told me she was alive during the first part of the *Biblical Exodus* and worshipped only one God whom her people, the Amo, called *El* and said it is the same God I know of but He is called by many names, and on other planets, He is called *'The Source'*.

During the mass exodus, she walked with her whole family and some of their livestock through Yam-Suf, which was Reed Lake but now called *Lake El Balah*. V told me it translates to "the lake where God devoured." She told me she died somewhere on the other side of that lake within days after that crossing. She said she watched from above as her father, who was a turquoise merchant, changed his mind about following Moses to the Promised Land but instead sold the livestock and took her family by boat to Greece, where he lived and died.

"Venus" – Bananarama (Lyrics)

Chapter 20

Ebony

One lifetime V told me about was when she lived around 4000 BCE and her name then was Ebony. I found out she lived somewhere near Egypt. Her entire head was always covered in many long braids. She had tiny beads in her dark brown hair. V told me she had to wear her hair that way. Otherwise, it was messy. It was thick and unmanageable with tight curls that knotted and stuck up in all directions.

She was outside most of the time and her skin tanned in the hot season but she was a lighter brown when the weather was cooler. Her pinky brown lips, brown eyes and thick black eyelashes that curled naturally towards her eyelids were the features of her face that made her look exceptionally beautiful.

She normally wore a handmade light brown goat-skin dress, which was short-sleeved and knee-length. The dress had multicoloured beads along the round neckline. V also owned two other dresses. One was made of multicoloured striped material and was only worn on special occasions. The other dress was similar to the goat-skin dress but this one was darker brown, and it didn't have beads on it. She told me, if the beaded dress were washed and hung out to dry, she would wear this one.

V continued, "I would bathe often in a small stream which ran nearby my house. This stream would also be used for our drinking water, cleaning clothes and cooking our food. Our livestock would gather by the bank and drink from this water too."

The houses she lived in were made of sand, stone, clay, and mud, which they would get from around the area and the banks of the River Nile about half a day's walk from where she lived. Her house was split-level, declining below the sand. It was cooler down there. She said she would enter her house through a cave-like entrance, which led to a spacious room above ground made of stone, mud, and clay.

When going down a few clay steps and slopes, there would be three much smaller, cooler and darker rooms below, entirely made with stone and clay from the river. There was no particular place her family used to sleep. The higher rooms would get very cold at night and hot during the day but the lower rooms were a nice constant temperature, which was perfect, as they used one of the lower rooms for animals that needed to be cared for.

There was another house next to hers that was similar and larger. Both houses were attached by a wooden roof. Here, food would be cooked and everyone would gather to eat in the evenings. The second house was built alongside hers. In one of the coolest rooms of that house, food was stored. This house was extended many times over, as and when they needed more rooms. V would live in both houses with her extended family.

The floors of the houses were packed with mud and they had holes in the walls for windows; animal skins would be spread over crossed wooden frames and placed on the windows only during storms. There was no furniture in the rooms, just neat piles of clothes, animal skin blankets and sleeping mats made of dried grass. The roofs were always covered with palm leaves, bundles of reeds and stones to protect it from the sun and rain. Sandstorms used to damage the houses often. Other family members were assigned to repair tasks and would have to fix it constantly and keep them maintained.

This was not the case with all her family members' and friends' dwellings. Some lived completely above the ground in other large communal places, like cities, with their extended families all together in stone houses. Some of V's family and friends lived in caves not far away from a smaller river that broke off from the Nile. V would visit them often with her parents and would stay there overnight before making the journey back home early the next morning.

"V, who did you live with and what did you do then?" I asked her.

"There were too many family members to count. I never learned how to count. I couldn't read or write either and I didn't know anyone who did! Only basic pictures were drawn. My sisters would crush up insects to use for coloured pictures but I didn't draw anything. I would rather weave animal bones or dried insects in between grasses, leaves and flowers to hang around my neck or waist. All the girls did that then," V replied. "I lived with my parents and recalling the faces of my siblings, we were ten siblings in total but not all lived with us. We never celebrated birthdays, so it's hard to tell everyone's ages but I'll try. Aunts, Uncles and their families lived with us too."

V said she was about 11 years old when she got sick and died and went on to tell me about the people she grew up with. She lived with many people, including her parents and her two sisters, who were identical twins. They were about 14 years old.

"Two of my older sisters, Bahiti and Akila, collected firewood, foraged for fruit, nuts, vegetables and berries for our whole family to eat. They would help to prepare the evening meals. We would all gather around a fire and eat outside on the floor together once a day. It was important that they knew how to cook good meals, because they were both preparing to leave home and be married. Kids got married exceedingly early then. We would eat out of coloured clay or stone bowls and cook flat shaped bread, fish and meat on fires just outside our home."

V continued, "My mother and I would look after and feed the noticeably young and sick animals. During that time, I was learning how to use local leaves and herbs to cure illnesses and diseases. These animals were kept inside, in pens within one of the rooms at the bottom of our house at night. Twice daily, we would collect untainted water for us all from far upstream and carry it back in pouches. While there, it was our job to feed the fowl that needed feeding, collect bird eggs on the ground and in between the marshes, which were near the stream. Outside, we looked after two pairs of breeding ostriches kept in pens and many ducks, pheasants and peacocks wandered our land freely. Milking the goats was also one of our many chores and when we were away on trips, all our chores were distributed among the family members left at home."

V's younger brothers, Omari and Sadiki, were aged nine and six, respectively, when V died. She said, "If not with my older brothers Asim and Ur, who would teach the boys how to attend goats nearby, my younger brothers would be looked after by my brothers' wives, Dalila and Khephi, during the day, at home with their own younger children."

V had two older brothers, Asim who was twenty-six and married to Dalila. Her older brother Ur was about 25 years old and was married to Khephi. If those brothers were not sleeping outside to watch over the goats, then they would sleep in the other house with Dalila and Khephi and their children.

V continued, "My mother's sisters, my Aunts Ife and Masika, would do everyone's laundry at the stream during the day. They'd do it together as it was a big task, then they would skin and prepare the food to cook in the evening. They both slept mostly in our house as the children were too noisy in the other one. My mother and Aunts were all local midwives, who would help babies to be born. They were hoping I would be one too but this never happened.

***

"The older females would take turns cooking and would teach the younger girls on most evenings, how to make items such as goat-skin clothes, baskets and sleeping mats to barter. Other family members lived close by and they grew wheat. My brother Asim would choose and exchange a few large bags of ground wheat for one of our small goats that he cared for when we ran out of flour to make bread. When the older men weren't doing their chores, they would teach the younger boys how to make fishing poles, tools and weapons. Everything that our group collected that we didn't eat or use, such as firewood, food, goat's milk and eggs, we would barter for things that we did need, and therefore, we all lived quite comfortably.

"Two of my father's younger brothers lived with us too, Uncle Chrisisi and Uncle Amon. Everyone had chores and jobs to do and we worked and survived as a family community. All three men worked together and did jobs like house, border fence and area maintenance. They hunted and fished. They made their own tools and dug holes around our borders for us to pee and poop in. My father and my two Uncles were away a lot. They hunted and fished and when home, they guarded everyone from wild animals. It seemed like every time my father returned home, soon after, my mother had another child!"

The rest of V's sisters had married and moved away to live with their husband's parents or were bartered as babies to good people who were friends of the family, in exchange for new animals.

"Our households used to breed the livestock we owned. There were not a lot of old people as they did not live as long as people these days. Our entire family lived in harmony," V said.

***

V told me about one of her trips and said, "My father, Uncle Chrisisi and Uncle Amon would leave two days before us to barter our home-made items and to fish on the River Nile. My mother and I would make that same journey by foot to the river the next day. We would take with us small round reed baskets my Aunties would make specially for our friends. These were gifts, our gratitude to them for accommodating us for the night spent there."

She said, eagerly recalling her past, "Mother would put those smaller gift baskets one inside another then would put that stack into a larger basket. She would fill it to the top with goat's milk, which were in skin pouches and many pieces of goat's meat and would carry that heavy basket on her head on the journey to see our friends. I would go along with her. The basket I would carry on my head was a little smaller than my mother's. It had fruits from the trees near our house: pomegranates, figs and berries. We journeyed there once a month. Just before we got there, we would unpack mother's large basket on the road and display the food nicely in the smaller gift baskets so when we arrive, our offering of thanks would look more presentable. We would be greeted by a big gathering of friends and that evening a feast would follow, with beer and cheap wine, even for the children!

"When we left our friends house the next morning for our journey home, I used to help carry back fish and seafood the men folk caught with my father to feed everyone back home for a few weeks. My mother and I would sometimes carry fish and other seafood in brine, sometimes covered in salt or packed mud from the riverbank, in the round handwoven reed baskets, which we originally brought with us, on our heads.

"Mine was a lot smaller than my mother's but still, it was heavy and my neck ached. My father and Uncles would follow us back a few days later with other items our community needed by bartering extra fish they had caught. Usually, he would exchange them with honey, cinnamon sticks, cumin seeds and other cooking spices. We didn't use money much, not like you do today. We exchanged goods. We weren't a rich family, Charm but we were not poor either," she said.

While walking home, V remembers being grabbed from behind. Some men stole their baskets. She saw her mother with her throat cut on the floor next to her. V was in pain and recalls lying down, going to sleep and seeing a light. The next thing she knew, she was walking in a beautiful place with her mother and other family members she had not seen for a while. V knew they were dead, and she was not scared.

"I went to heaven!" she said and went on to tell me she had been studying a lot and had been training to be a guardian for me, for fifteen lifetimes to many other people before me, for this lifetime. V has walked the earth many times throughout the ages and has lived on hundreds of other beautiful planets.

"Ebony and Ivory" – Paul McCartney and Stevie Wonder (Lyrics)

Max, V and Me
would like to thank you for reading this book.

We present you with a bonus chapter
and hope you continue to follow
Charm's journey as she grew up.

Until we meet again,
we send you love, joy and peace.

Chapter 21

Winnie

*I*n one of many lifetimes, V lived to the age of one or two in London. The year was 1870. She had blue eyes and blond hair and her name was Mary Winifred Warner but her mother called her Winnie. She was drowned in the River Fleet, which flowed near her home, by her mother who was unmarried, poor and not well in the head. She does not remember much of that life, the Moment of her death or the light but she does remember growing up in heaven and is happy being a guardian here on earth.

"Why did you have to die at such a young age?" I asked V.

She told me she had to learn in that lifetime what it was like to be starved and to experience physical abuse, so when she became a guardian, she would know how the person she is guarding feels. She told me the best part of that life was learning how to walk and talk. The rest of that life was really painful.

She said I was the first person she has been guarding who can actually hear what she is saying and the only person alive who knows what she really looks like, her true form. She has never guarded anyone who has a guide assigned, that will converse with the human before but in school within the heavenly realm, she learned about guardians that have. That is why she wanted this mission with me. V told me Max and she gets on really well.

"V, are there many people like me that can see and hear spirits?" I asked.

"Yes," she replied. "There are a lot more people like you than you think, Charm. All throughout time past, there are thousands here in the present and there will be more people to come, most definitely in the future!"

"So . . . V, when did we first meet?" I once asked her.

"We first met in heaven. Our paths have crossed many times throughout space and within different dimensions, we used to know each other very well," she replied.

"Drift Away" – Uncle Kracker (Lyrics)

Glossary Of Characters

Character	How they relate to me
Adam Slayer (my Uncle and godfather)	Married to Edna
Andrew Trudy	Married my Mom's sister Jess
Anthony (Tony) Sweets	My brother, one year older than me
Antoinette	One of my best friends
Baxter Slayer	My male cousin; Jen's brother; he is five years younger than Jen and me
Bindu Luv	My cousin, my Dad's niece from India
Bobby (my Uncle Bo)	(Grey Army Man) One of my Dad's younger brothers
Charm (me)	Maiden Name: Sweets
Daniel Baker (my Uncle Danny)	Married my Mom's sister Rose
Edna Slayer (my Auntie and godmother)	My Mom's eldest sister; married to Adam Slayer; together, they had two kids: Jen and Baxter Slayer
Everyone else	Fill-in people, including medical people
Gary Thompson	Was, at first, married to my Auntie Jane; between them, they had Gaz Jr., Lea and Si Thompson
Gary Jr. (Gaz) Thompson	My eldest male cousin, four years older than me
Grandfather (Grandpa) Stephen Copper	My Mom's father, married to Rosemary

Grandmother (Nana) Rosemary Copper	Married to Stephen Copper; together, they had six kids, namely, in birth order, Edna, Jane, Marg (my Mom), Jess, Bob (their only son) and Rose
Hector (teddy bear)	My best friend and confidant
Helen Chance (remarkably close friend of ours, the Sweets, the Coppers, the Bakers and the Thompson families)	Whom I called "Auntie;" she had a kid, Tammy Chance, We would often spend time together
Ignatius Sweets	My father (Dad)
Jane Frost (my Auntie Jane)	My Mom's second sister; was married to Gary Sr. Thompson then married Rusty Frost; mother to Gaz Jr., Lea and Si
Jessica Trudy (my Auntie Jess)	My mother's first younger sister; she was married to Andrew; together, they had three kids: my cousins Amanda, Kelly and Dawn
Leanne (Lea) Thompson	My eldest female cousin, three years older than me; she had a boyfriend, John, who was a photographer
Leslie	My husband
Margorie (Marg) Sweets	My mother (Mom)
Marisha (Mari)	My best friend since OG Elementary
Maximillian (Max)	My guide angel
Mick	Lodger: we dated for a month or so
Michael	My baby son
Ms Parker	One of my many high school teachers
Neena (Nee)	My best friend since OG Elementary
Raj	My first real boyfriend
Ray	A person I dated a few times when I was sixteen; we met again later while working at MW advertising agency
Robert Copper (my Uncle Bob)	My Mom's only brother, the second youngest in the Copper family; he also married and had kids

Rose Baker (my Auntie Rose)	My Mom's youngest sister, the last of four sisters and a brother; she was married to Uncle Danny; together, they had three kids: Alison, Mark and Patricia Baker
Rusty Sr Frost	Married to my Auntie Jane; together, they had three more of my younger cousins
Sandi	My first friend at SJM School
Simon (Si) Thompson	My cousin, one year older than me
Sir Isaac Copper	One of my ancestors on my Mom's side of the family going back to the 1600s
Theresa (Terry) Sweets	My sister, four years younger than me
Venus (V)	My guardian angel
Veronica	My nan's sister whom I called "Auntie"

"Tell me and I forget,
Teach me and I remember,
Involve me and I learn."

Benjamin Franklin

Song Dedications

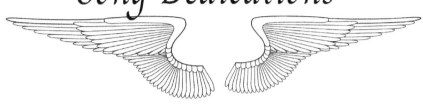

*(I found these songs free on YouTube in 2023. You can
purchase to ensure royalties go to those talented artists.)*

Chapter, Songs and Dedications
Chapter 1   The Gift
"Chiquitita" – Abba (Lyrics) (Tiktok Song)
(From V to me)

Chapter 2   Max, V and Me
"When You Believe" – Whitney Houston and Mariah Carey (Lyrics)
(From Max to me)

Chapter 5   My Early Family
"Danny Boy" – GENTRI Covers (Lyrics)
(For Grandpa)

Chapter 6   Early School Years
"No One" – Alicia Keys (Lyrics)
(From me to Max and V)

Chapter 7   Bonfire
"He Ain't Heavy, He's My Brother" – The Hollies (Lyrics)
(For my brother Tony)

Chapter 8   The House on Springfield Gardens
"Green, Green Grass of Home" – Tom Jones (Lyrics)
(For my Auntie Jane)

*Max, V and I thank all the musical artists we have mentioned in this book.
Without their songs, we genuinely believe that my life would be unbearable.
We believe your songwriting skills, voices and musical talents are gifts
from God! Thank you all again for sharing your talents with the world.*

Testimony

This is the testimonial of Charm's mother, known as Marjorie Sweets in the Max, V and Me series of books.

I testify that I recall the scenes Charm had described throughout this book. I went through every chapter with her and I remember most of the things she has written about. While reading through the book with her remotely, proof-copying chapters for Charm and while recently on Messenger's video calls, many years have drifted by as she had tried writing the Max, V and Me books over multiple decades to eventually publish them for future generations of our family.

While reading draft copies of her book and listening to her words as she read, describing scenes from the past, took me back to those days I recall I had actually taken part in. It was sometimes during parts of her lifetime when I spoke to Charm on a regular basis over the phone, about the things as they were troubling her and unfolding, in actual time that had occurred and was recalled and documented truthfully within the chapters of this book. Sometimes we discussed me recalling a slightly different perspective from Charm but it was virtually what I could recall too.

There are also some things Charm had kept secret from me and the world until it was time to reveal information. I understand now why she was behaving the way she was when young. Sometimes I could not get through to her as much as I tried but now, as we are discussing our supernatural gifts together, our relationship is much better and closer as mother and daughter. I read through these periods also with her and we have spoken about those chapters in detail. I believe what she has written, as I also have a supernatural gift and sometimes struggle with it. I do not want to talk about my gift though. However, I know what she is saying is true.

I believe in Max and V, that they exist and are not evil entities, also that they were born to help my daughter through her life's journey. I understand completely why sometimes it is hard to believe supernatural events, but just because you don't believe it, it doesn't mean that the event didn't happen. Keeping this in mind, I hope that you enjoy the book. Like Charm, I too hope it helps some people. I love my Charm very much . . . more than words can say. She is so special to me. Read her book, and you will understand her as a kindhearted and caring person.

Max, V and Me

The Continued Journey

Book 2

Chapters 22 to 42

Library of Congress Control Number: 2023907293
Max, V and Me.
The Continued Journey.
ISBN: Hardcover 979-8-3694-9115-7
Softcover 979-8-3694-9114-0
eBook 979-8-3694-9113-3

Max, V and Me

Troubled Times

Book 3

Chapters 43 to 63

Index

Printed in Great Britain
by Amazon

30784815R00091